Be A Winning Coach

Robin Clarkson

*We at Trafford believe that it is the responsibility of us all, as both individuals
and corporations, to make choices that are environmentally and socially sound.
You, in turn, are supporting this responsible conduct each time you purchase a
Trafford book, or make use of our publishing services. To find out how you are
helping, please visit www.trafford.com/responsiblepublishing.html*

*Our mission is to efficiently provide the world's finest, most comprehensive
book publishing service, enabling every author to experience success.
To find out how to publish your book, your way, and have it available
worldwide, visit us online at www.trafford.com*

Trafford rev.11/16/2009

 www.trafford.com

North America & international
toll-free: 1 888 232 4444 (USA & Canada)
phone: 250 383 6864 ♦ fax: 812 355 4082 ♦ email: info@trafford.com

*The more you
know and understand*

*The simpler and more effective
you can make it.*

Contents

Part 2

Grow a Winning Organization

Part 3

Attain Your Aims

Introduction

Over the years I've had many discussions with people who coach at an international, regional and club level and who coach a variety of sports, including rugby, soccer, netball, cricket, basketball, tennis, bowls, judo and field hockey. From these discussions, **what comes across is a perception that the sport they coach is different to others**, mainly because of the skills and technical attributes associated with each.

After talking with coaches, contrary to the perceptions, **I am constantly struck by how much each sport and each level has in common,** and if you talk to enough successful coaches from different sports and begin analyzing what they say and do, you start to see **the principles to be a winning coach and for preparing a winning side and winning individual, are the same.** This is regardless of the players' age, organisation size or level competing at.

Also when coaching, you are dealing with a paradox for ultimately you've got to get results if you want to be taken seriously or as a professional coach, to keep your job. To get results, you have to get better. To get better you have try things. If you try things, you'll make mistakes, there is no avoiding them. Unfortunately sport is a place which doesn't tolerate too many mistakes, especially the higher up you go. This is where the paradox comes into play because **you want to get results and get better, but if you try things, you may not get the results and improvements you are after.**

This book has come about because of this very paradox, for **if you know the principles to succeed, you can train for success.**

In coaching, I've made plenty of mistakes, some at the wrong time, which has cost me games and places at tournaments. I've also learnt, improved and applied what I have discovered. From my experiences and research, I've come to a greater understanding of the coaching process and there is one fundamental truth I have come across. **If coaches want to prepare a winning team or winning individual, they need to know how to bake a cake.** The reason being, the four steps you need to bake a cake are the same steps you need to follow for putting together a winning team and individual.

To help guide you along the coaching process this book is in three parts, and I've included exercises that will clarify your thinking and help to develop your own coaching method; for everyone has got different strengths and styles they work to.

Part one explores what you need to know to be a winning coach and follows the baking analogy for preparing a winning team. Though the focus is on the team, the same principles apply to individuals. I also deal with real world situations which are compiled from my own experiences and observations that occur in sport and which happen during games and tournaments.

Part two is for anyone wishing to put together a winning sports organisation and deals with how the administration, umpires, coaches and the players must work together to succeed. It also provides common sense guidelines to help an organisation to develop and reach the top.

Part three looks at the process that goes into reaching your aims and getting better.

This book has taken me too many places and to explore many areas of the sporting setup, which very few have delved into or even thought about up until now. It has also taken me on a journey to a destination I didn't know I would reach but have been grateful for taken that path. The beauty of this whole philosophy is that you can apply it to any endeavour you wish to get involved in and end up being successful at what ever level you wish to achieve.

You could spend years finding out what it takes to be a winning coach, or you can take the short cut and use the information contained within these pages.

In everything you do there are always two options. You can either set yourself up for failure or set yourself up for success. The choice is yours.

This book is designed to set you up for success.

Part 1

The Winning Philosophy

Any person can complicate the simple.

Few look to simplify the complicated.

Be a
Winning Coach

Without any trust

You can not build a
consistent winning team

What does it take to be a winning coach?

That's a question I asked myself for many years. I've been to a lot of coaching clinics in which a majority of them were based around the sports skills and how to prepare a training session, which means people were getting and having access to the same information.

If that was the case, then **why was it that only some coaches were doing all the winning, but a majority of coaches were not?** There had to be more.

Having piqued my interest, I had to find out. So I set myself the task of uncovering, **what do winning coaches work from that the majority of coaches don't?** I wanted to know the answer because I wanted to become a winning coach myself. I didn't realize the quest to answer this question was going to take me 20 years.

After studying, observing, talking to other coaches, asking questions, gathering information, heading down blind alley ways, coming back, trialing, experimenting and sorting through what I had, I then correlated all the information and arrived at five essentials that winning coaches work from that puts them ahead of everyone else.

The five essentials that winning coaches work from are:

They have an aim and a picture of what they want to achieve on the playing field

They have a list of key skills and know their techniques

They get the best out of their players

They have a brain for their sport

They have a recipe or a method for putting it all together

By following and working from these five points, winning coaches set themselves up for success.

It's not the only things they do, winning coaches also have three ideals they work from and aim for when preparing their team to go onto the field. They are:

The type of game they aim to get their team to play is **a Positive Flowing game.**

The style of game they aim to play through the midfield is a **Controlled Short Passing game.**

The type of players they develop are **Class Skillful Thinking Players.**

Behaviour also forms an essential part of winning coaches and they look for and develop three things in themselves as well as looking to instill these qualities in their players.

The three qualities are:

Excellence

Standards

Improvement

All of a sudden when looking at the information, it can be seen why an effective winning coach can take years to develop and produce.

What I have said doesn't mean winning coaches will gain winning results 100% of the time. **What winning coaches will be doing, is working to the principles for success, striving for their aims and be looking to have a 70 to 80% win ratio to give themselves a chance to win a seasons competition, for that's what it takes to be a winning coach.**

To win a tournament, you need a 90 to 100% win ratio.

This book is about the principles to be a winning coach and to get you started on the path; we'll begin with the five essentials they work from.

Have an Aim and a Picture

How many coaches have an aim and a picture of what they are heading towards on the sports field?

My guess is very few. Having an aim and a picture of what you want to achieve on the playing field is an area of sport which is given very little attention, yet has such a big impact on what people will achieve with their coaching. **To show you the importance of having an aim and a picture,** when you build a house you have a blue print of what it is going to turn out like.

When you begin a journey, or go on a trip, you have a destination you are aiming to reach. By having a description or picture of the destination, you will know when you have arrived or more importantly know if you going off track and moving away from where you are heading.

Like wise, if you are saving money, you give yourself a total to reach, and then when you achieve the target, you can either spend it or you could go, I could save more, so you adjust the amount to save to a higher figure.

By now I hope you see the importance of having an aim and a picture of what you want to achieve because **one of the keys to any winning coach is to have**

an aim and a picture of what you want to achieve on the playing field and
have it written down. By having it written down, this helps to develop clarity
in what you want to achieve. For without clarity your results will be hazy and
non descript.

If you reach your on field aim and picture and you think you could do better,
or think your team could play a better style and type of game, you adjust the
aim and picture to help you reach higher and gain better results. This aim
and picture adjustment is an on going process as you will always find ways to
get better, though the basic principles of what you are trying to achieve may
remain the same.

If you are unable to see the importance of having an aim and a picture,
you will not achieve the results you may desire.

Know your key skills

If you know the key skills for your sport and the correct techniques for
executing them, then you will be effective as a coach. By knowing the key
skills, you can focus on what to teach and give your players a good base to
work from. To clarify, there is a difference between basic skills and key
skills.

In field hockey the basic skills are hitting the ball, pushing the ball, receiving
the ball and dribbling the ball, but are they the key skills? Key skills are the
ones that make the biggest difference to the performance of your team out of
all of the others?

For example, when hitting the hockey ball you can either box hit, sweep hit,
reverse hit or tomahawk hit, which one is the key skill?

When receiving the hockey ball, you can reverse stick trap, forehand trap or
upright trap, which one is the key skill?

Some of your key skills will not come from the basics of your sport. You also have to look behind the obvious basic skills to uncover more key skills and their techniques.

For example, when goal scoring is it the skills you use to score goals that is the key or the techniques you use for setting up to score goals? Is it when you have the ball or what you do when you don't have the ball that is the key?

One way to determine a key skill is if you take away that skill, you do not perform with the same effectiveness and it affects your standard of play. Working out the key skills has been the unlocking of the door for me to become a winning coach and raise the standard of my players. For others it could be learning how to get the best out of people.

Also knowing the skills techniques, when you practice, rather than just doing the drills to keep players occupied, you combine the drills with executing the correct techniques, in effect doing two practices in one.

By doing the key skills and their techniques at practice, you are conditioning your players to do them in a game.

Get the best out of your players

If you are unable to or do not know how to get the best out of your players, do not be frustrated with the lack of results, because you won't get any or at best, very few. Like developing the aim and picture, actively getting the best out of players is something little attention is paid to.

When working to get the best out of your players, questions to ask yourself would include:

* **How do you mould your team together?**

* **Are they playing well because they want to** or because they have to?

* **Are you working from a positive perspective** or negative?

* **Are you building your players up** or breaking them down?

* **Are you motivating by encouragement** or antagonizing?

* **Are you building harmony into your side** or disharmony?

* **Are you focusing on players' strengths** or weaknesses?

* **Do the players trust your training methods?**

* **Do the players trust you as a person?**

I've seen people coaching teams to get their own kids ahead at the expense of children with better talent and then turning around wondering why they've got disharmony in the team, losing players and not getting results and then becoming defensive if you want to talk about how to improve their coaching. I guess their chances of being a winning coach are pretty slim unless they change their approach to coaching.

Getting the best out of your players is an important part of the coaching process and is integral to any success.

Have a brain for your sport

If you develop an intermit knowledge of your sport, you can really plan, progress and develop. If you want to have a brain for your sport some of the things you need to work on, develop and improve are:

* **Know the rules of the game**

* **Game scenarios**

* **Game analysis**

* **Player analysis**

* **Tactical appreciation**

* **Know how to win**

* **Know how to plan to win**

* **Know how to read the play**

* **Know the make up of your sport**

* **Understand the subtleties of your sport**

* **Understand player development**

* **Know the skills for your sport**

* **Know the key skills for your sport**

* **Know what works and what doesn't work**

If you develop all of the above points, people will seem to think you have this sixth sense and intuition, whereas in reality it is an intermit knowledge and understanding of your sport and how things work.

Having a brain for your sport you develop an understanding of your game and when to take the appropriate action.

Have a method for putting it all together

How do you put it all together to get consistent on field results or do you Just wing it and hope it all turns out for the best? One thing I tell my players is, if I can't explain why we are doing something at practice and what it is going to achieve, we shouldn't be doing it. By saying this, it challenges me to know what I am doing.

Things you will have to consider when putting together your trainings are:

* How long have you got to work with the team?

* Are you targeting a season, a tournament or a series?

* How many practices do you have?

* How do you structure your practices?

* When do you start?

* What do you have to work on?

* When do they need to be worked on?

* When do you peak for?

* When do you start tapering?

As you can appreciate by now, being a winning coach and coaching a winning sports team isn't just about going to a few coaching clinics, learning the sports skills and finding how to organize practices.

What I've found is if you ask question after question after question to develop your understanding, the answers will eventually come that will take you to your aim, for the better the aim, the higher the standards, the better the execution, the greater the results.

If you have a method for putting it all together, and know how everything interacts, you can replicate winning results.

Based on the previous five pages, here are six questions you need to ask yourself and be able to answer so you can become a winning coach.

* Do I want to be a successful coach who prepares and produces winning teams on the sports field?

* What is the aim and picture I have for playing on the sports field that will enable the sides I take to become winning teams?

* What are the key skills for my sport which my players need to have, to enable them to succeed?

* How am I actively working to get the best out of my players and what am I doing to create harmony within the side?

* What knowledge do I possess about my sport, and do I know how everything interacts together?

* What is my method or recipe I am working from to be able to put everything together, and how do I go about doing it?

Irrespective of what team you are taking, or the standard of the team, or the level being played or the abilities of the players, these six questions will always remain the same, as they are the basis for becoming a winning coach.

After you read the next section and go through the exercises, you will be able to provide your own answers to all of the questions, which will set you on the path to becoming a winning coach who prepares winning teams.

Prepare a Winning Team

Work the process to attain the aim

The Link between Baking and Sport

Two weeks after coming back from an under 16 girls National Hockey Tournament, I was sitting with some of the parents at our teams dinner, and towards the end of the evening, for some reason, the conversation got round to baking cakes. Somewhere in the middle of the discussion about baking, my mind made the link between the steps you take for making a cake, compared to putting together a sports team and the similarities between the two.

When I made the connection, straight away I said to myself, **how to bake a cake would be a great analogy for explaining to people how to put together a winning team.**

Like anything I do, when I get thoughts coming through my head, I grabbed a pen and paper and wrote down a few notes so I wouldn't lose the idea. I'm always amazed how the mind can link two seemingly unrelated areas together, find the common thread and then come up with an analogy to be able to explain it.

Running with this baking analogy, **let's begin the process for putting together a winning team.**

When you decide to make a cake, you first have to make up your mind on which one you are going to bake.

Cakes you may choose from include:

* Chocolate cake

* Fruit cake

* Xmas cake

* Banana cake

* Carrot cake

You pick one and that's your starting point.

It's the same with sport; for whatever reason, you may get involved to coach:

* Field Hockey

* Football (soccer)

* Rugby

* Netball

* Gaelic Football

* Any other sport you can think of

It doesn't matter which cake you decide to bake or sport you end up coaching, **the steps and basic principles for putting together both for success, are the same.**

From here on in, to keep consistency through out, I'll be using field hockey as the example and showing how **the four steps for baking a cake will help you prepare a winning team.**

We'll now work our way through each of the four steps for preparing a winning team.

Step 1
The Picture

After deciding which cake you are going to make or sport you are going to coach, **you will need a picture of the final product you are aiming for.** What the picture does is gives you a reference point and an aim on which you are directing your efforts towards. For some reason, we ignore the picture and aim of what we would like to see happen on the field and go straight to working with the sports skills.

There is more to coaching than just teaching skills. Like any good project, you must have a starting point.

The starting point for anyone coaching should be what is the aim and picture I'm working towards on the field and what it will look like, for **without an aim, you have no focus. With no focus, you get no strong results.**

What is an aim?

An aim is the target you are heading for and they can be anything.

There are four types of aims.

The three common aims are:

* **A long term aim**

* **A medium term aim**

* **A short term aim**

The fourth aim is:

* **A playing aim**

The **long term aim** will be something that is way off in the distance.

The **medium term aim** is an aim you need to reach to be able to attain your long term aim.

The **short term aim** will be something the players have to improve upon and they can be many.

The **playing aim** is the least understood of the four and is what your team is trying to achieve, as a unit, when on the field.

Here is all four aims in a practical example, though your own aims will be different, depending on the sport played and the teams coached.

Playing aim:

The teams I coach, I want them to play the best type of game they can

Long term aim:

To win a national tournament

Medium term aim:

To make the top six at a national tournament

Short term aims:

To improve players receiving skills
To improve players passing accuracy
To get all players to communicate more on the field

Your long, medium and short term aims will change as your players and teams get better, or you swap teams to take on new challenges.

The playing aim will change very little as you can shift it from team to team because it will be your ultimate driving force. That's why I've put it at the top of the example.

The playing aim is the one we'll focus on, as the other three are covered at length by most sports.

The playing aim is the foundation stone on which everything is built and when you decide on your playing aim, you then have to develop the picture to achieve that aim.

It is worth putting time into the consideration of your playing aim for **the better the playing aim, the better the picture you will develop for what you want to happen on the field.** The drive of any winning coach is in the pursuit of excellence and **the way to achieve excellence on the field is to play the best type of game you can.**

When it comes to the picture, it will not be the tactical day to day stuff you will look at; rather it will be a picture of an ideal of what you would like to see happen on the field, based on your playing aim.

Do not get me wrong. When it comes to each game, the tactical side is important and how you negate the opposition play and their tactics, though, if you want to lift yourself above the pack and become dominant, then **your ideal picture for the playing aim is crucial because it gives you a standard you are constantly striving towards.**

When it comes to baking, you look through a cook book and find a physical picture of what you are going to attempt. With sport it's not so simple. There is no book you can flick through and find a picture of what you are going to create. Therefore you have to build the picture up with words. One way to develop your picture for your playing aim is to look at how the very successful sides are playing in any sport.

To build this picture you have to look at:

* **The type of game you want to play**

* **The style of game you want to play**

* **The type of player you want to develop**

* The way you want to play on the field

Let's look at each of the four areas by looking at what the very successful sides do, so you can build your picture.

The Type of Game

It all started for me as a 12 year old while watching the Liverpool football side of the 1978 – 79 season. Their type and style of game captivated me and they were also very successful.

It was brilliant to watch and seemed so natural and easy and has had a big effect on my own playing and subsequent coaching development. They always seemed to play this flowing type of game and from that point on, I watched other sides that are very successful and **the flowing game keeps coming to the fore.**

Field Hockey's International body has it written into their rule book, under their umpire guidance section, and reads, **that umpires must apply the advantage rule as much as possible to assist a flowing and open match but without losing control.**

Subsequently in my research I have found that there are only really two types of game you can play, the positive flowing game or the negative slow down, disrupt and stop the opposition game.

The Style of Game

The style of game refers to how you are going to get the ball through the midfield.

* Is this part of your game going to be an individual affair when players get the ball and just run with it?

* Is it going to be achieved with moving the ball over a long distance between players?

* Is it going to be a once touch and deflection game, played as though the ball is a hot potato?

* Is it going to be a controlled short passing?

With all the successful teams I've watched and from my own experience, **the controlled short passing game through the midfield stands out head and shoulders above everything else.** Occasionally the very successful teams have resorted to other styles of game when the tactics or situations arise, but their over riding aim is for the short passing game.

The Type of player you want to develop

I've looked at a lot of sport over the years and the top sports people always display the same type of attributes, regardless of the sport they play. They are what I term to be **class skillful thinking** players.

A class skillful thinking player is someone who does the basics well, is very skillful, is game smart and mentally tough.

The secret to a class skillful thinking player is you never really see how skillful they are. These players are always putting themselves in a position to use their basics, but if they need to, will use their skills when required.

If during a game they do not use their skill, it's not a big issue; maybe the game didn't warrant it.

During a game, class skillful thinking players are always looking to create opportunities or waiting for opportunities, sometimes by not doing things in a game, e.g. they keep passing the ball and create opportunities as the opposition markers drift off them to start covering the pass and then start leaving holes in their defence. Class skillful thinking players then pounce and use their skills to exploit the holes in defence. In tight games such as quarters, semis and finals, these opportunities may occur only once or twice in a whole game.

The difference between a class skillful thinking player and someone who is just as talented but not reaching the same heights, can be summed up in four words, **Self Discipline** and **Mental Maturity.** What self discipline and mental maturity gives these players is the ability to do the same things over and over again without getting bored and drifting off to something else. **Because these players have self discipline and mental maturity, they can apply themselves to the task at hand.**

The following are the different parts of a class skillful thinking player. Most coaches tend to only focus on teaching the skills of the sport and hope a person with the attributes to be a class player turns up.

Class in players

We can all pick a class player or point to a class team but can have trouble when we have to say what defines it. Here is a quick check list to look for and help identify class players:

* Soft hands

* Quick hands (feet in soccer)

* Appear to have time

* Makes a skill look easy and effortless

* Hand eye co ordination and timing

* Always thinking ahead of the play

* Does not show all of their skill all the time

* Puts themselves in a position to perform the basics

* Neat and crisp in executing skills

* Able to perform under pressure

Skillful in players

This is associated with hand eye, feet eye and body co ordination.

If you can find ways to develop these co ordination attributes, then your players will become more skillful.

Thinking in players

Thinking is a very important part of the game. Some skillful players aren't as proficient in this section of the game. The areas involved in the thinking process are:

Games Scenarios:

How good are players at recognizing game scenarios during a game?

Structual play:

Are they able to do the same job in the position they are playing over and over again or do they go off on a tangent and get caught out of position on a regular basis?

Read the play:

Know what is going to occur before it happens, by looking at the clues to what is taking place around them, E.g. Body language, ebb and flow of the game, what the opposition are trying to do.

Reading the play is closely aligned with structural play. Are players able to look at what is happening, and be able to put themselves in a position before it happens, or to cut off options for the opposition?

Communicates on the field:

Are players able to see what is happening or needs to be done and can they communicate this to their team mates or are they part of the silent service.

Knows the games rules:

If you are going to play a sport, the more you know the rules, the more effective you can be.

Mental toughness:

If you come up against set backs or things aren't going the way you would like them to, to have the mental strength to work through and get back up if you have been knocked down, both physically and mentally.

The way you want to play on the field

In looking at the way you want to play, you have to ask your self such questions as:

* When do we create width, height or depth?

* When do we create congestion?

* How do we work for goal or point scoring opportunities?

* How do we deny the opposition goal or point scoring opportunities?

* Are we playing as individuals or as a unit?

* Have we the ability to communicate?

* What sort of structure are we playing defensively and in attack?

The questions you can come up with in this part is endless and depends on how and what you want to achieve on the field and the restrictions enforced by the rules of the game you are involved in.

We'll now shift onto the first exercise to begin the process for preparing a winning team, but first you need to write down your playing aim.

For example, my playing aim for the teams I coach is to play the best type of hockey they can. Now complete the following sentence to state your playing aim.

My playing aim for the teams I coach is ......

As an example of a picture, based on my playing aim, here is the picture for what we want to achieve on the playing field in the sport of field hockey.

* We are playing a flowing game, with accurate passing through the midfield. (Passing game between the 25's) If I haven't got the ball I am making myself available for passes.

* We are moving the ball across the field away from congestion, especially after gaining a turnover and we have the ability to switch the play at any time.

* We are organized in defence and attack and there is plenty of communication on the field in letting each other know what is happening, by either directing traffic or calling for the ball.

* We are creating many goal scoring opportunities during the game which we put away efficiently either by ourselves or with the use of our team mates, by using the correct techniques inside the circle.

* We are taking our penalties quick and when defending penalties, are setting up quicker than the opposition is taking theirs.

* We are creating width and space when we have the ball and creating congestion when the opposition has the ball.

* We are showing desperation in defence and aggression in attack to get the ball, for the whole game.

* We are working as a unit when we are on the field, playing structurally in both attack and defence.

* We are skillful players who are adept at executing the basics of field hockey with the correct techniques, to a high standard.

* We are game smart and mentally tough enough to combat and react to any situation that is occurring on the field.

* We take pride in the way we play and practice and act in the manner befitting that of a quality sports person.

Now it's your turn to develop your picture. **For the first exercise, to build your picture** based on your playing aim, write down what an ideal game would be like for your sport.

Name the type of game you would like to play:

Name the style of game that you would like to play through the midfield:

Name the type of player you would like to develop:

What attributes do the best players in your sport display?

1:

2:

3:

4:

5:

6:

7:

Identify how you would want to play on the field, what would be your ideal game:

1:

2:

3:

4:

5:

6:

7:

8:

9:

10.

When you have completed this exercise, you will have a picture of what you are working towards on the playing field.

We've covered the aim and the picture, the second step focuses on the skills and attributes your players need, that will enable you to start achieving the picture you have developed.

Without an aim
you have no focus

With no focus
you get no strong results

Step 2
The Ingredients

When baking a cake, there are two types of ingredients that you require.

The first is a set of **dry ingredients** and these form the basis of your cake. These ingredients include things such as flour, sugar, salt and baking powder.

The second set you need is **wet ingredients**, such as milk, water and eggs. These help to bind your dry ingredients together.

It's the same principle for putting together a sports team.

You need a set of **dry ingredients**. These ingredients form the basis of your sport. They are your **sports basic/key skills, skill level** (e.g. hand eye co-ordination), **thinking and fitness.**

You also need **wet ingredients** which you use to bind your team together. They are **self discipline, commitment** and **harmony.**

Baking	**Sport**
Dry Ingredients (Forms basis of cake)	*Dry Ingredients* (Forms basis of sport)
* Flour	* Basics/key skills
* Sugar	* Skill Level
* Salt	* Thinking
* Baking Powder	* Fitness
Wet Ingredients (Binds dry ingredients)	*Wet Ingredients* (Binds team together)
* Milk	* Self Discipline
* Water	* Commitment
* Eggs	* Harmony

Therefore, when putting together a winning team, the seven areas to look at and work on, are:

* Basic/Key skills

* Skill level

* Thinking

* Fitness

* Self Discipline

* Commitment

* Harmony

By measuring your team against these seven areas, you can work out what you can target to improve your team.

As a quick sideline, **you can equate this coaching concept to the nuts, bolts and washers which hold up a yachting mast.** When everything's working right, they sit there in the open and no one pays them any attention. When they fail, you know about it.

Unlike the yachting mast, the nuts, bolts and washers of success for sporting organisations are hidden. They get lost in the clutter as people complicate issues with petty politics, empire building and personal egos and if people have a closed mind, this coaching concept can be easily dismissed. The reason being, **these are the simple basic building blocks to success,** and what I have found is they are the things that get brushed aside in peoples rush for control.

Having an open mind enables you to challenge your own thinking and beliefs and for most people this is quite scary, as it may expose the foundations their beliefs are built upon.

As in life, it is the simple basic information you implement and work at that gives you the best results. You need an understanding of the complex issues but **without an understanding of the base you'll never have a solid foundation to work from. Let's continue.**

Every team you coach will present new challenges as the makeup of the players will determine the initial strengths and weaknesses of the team. A change in two or three players can change the makeup and composition of the seven areas.

One side that I had, which went onto become a winning team, their initial makeup, highlighted by the bold lettering, was:

* Basic/Key skills

* Skill level

* Thinking

* Fitness

* Self Discipline

* **Commitment**

* **Harmony**

After working with them for a season, the team makeup became:

* Basic/Key skills

* **Skill level**

* Thinking

* **Fitness**

* **Self Discipline**

* Commitment

* Harmony

As can be seen from this example, the team changed over the season, so as a coach you have to keep evaluating your team for the changes as people improve or come and go from the team.

Also as you rise higher, if you try putting together a sports team by leaving out some of the seven areas, you won't be as successful as you could be. We'll now work our way through each of the seven areas to find and isolate the key components of each.

Dry Ingredients

As previously mentioned, these ingredients form the basis of your sport, without these you would not be able to play your sport to the best of your ability. The ingredients you eventually identify will stem back to the picture you have for what you are trying to achieve. It is no use using ingredients which won't go towards achieving your aim on the field.

Sports Basics/Key skills

The sports basics and key skills are the very minimum needed to compete successfully in your sport. It's generally going to be between 4 to 10 skills peculiar to your sport.

You will need to look at:

* The skills required to receive the ball or object, and to move or pass the ball or object on

* A players body position and hand or feet positions

* How you score goals or scoring points

* How you gain possession

* How you defend

Some of the key skills you may find important, which others may not deem so crucial.

The more you get to understand your sport, the better you will identify what the valuable key skills are.

Skill Level

This is the flash stuff that people do. Revolves around hand eye co-ordination, hand feet co ordination and body movement.

If you can come up with drills and ways to improve these, then a players ability to compete at a higher level will rise. Sometimes it can be a simple technique adjustment which will help with players co-ordination abilities or have to work on actual co ordination exercises.

Thinking

Sport isn't just about turning up and running around. Players need to understand the game they are playing, how to work as a unit and be able to communicate on the field.

Game Scenarios:

If you have got answers to what is happening or can recognize situations or the ebb and flow that is happening on the field, then you can react and change them a lot quicker. E.g. During a game, rather than waiting until afterwards.

Structual Play:

* How does your team operate in both defence and attack, what role does each position play?

* Is everyone playing to the same structure?

* Does everyone know the role of each position?

One lesson learnt at my very first tournament as a coach was, if your team doesn't **play to a structure**, you're going to be eaten up by the opposition as your players try to cover each other rather than performing a role, and your players will be tired by the business end of a tournament when they need to be performing at their best.

Read the Play:

It comes down to the ability to constantly ask your self two key questions all the time during the game.

For Defence

* Where is the opposition likely to attack and for the position I am playing, am I currently in the right place to help stop that potential attack.

* Before I receive the ball, whether that is from a tackle, pass or intercept, what is my next available pass?

And if you get really good, where is the person I pass the ball too going to pass next?

For Attack

* Where is the best position for me to receive the ball?

* When I do get the ball what am I going to do with it?

Three other questions to ask, irrespective of the position played, are, where's the space, where's my team mates, where's the opposition.

In reality that's all there is to reading the play. As with most things, the simplest concepts can be the hardest to implement.

Communicates on the Field:

Communication is the life blood to both attack and defence. If everyone in your team belongs to the silent service, and do not communicate, how is anyone going to know what is happening? If a team is working well defensively, you can guarantee that they will be communicating.

Communication isn't just mindless chatter, Players generally use key words such as: hold, got you covered, I've got ball, you go forward, watch high man, player coming across, run your channels.

Knows the Games Rules:

Pretty much self explanatory, if you know the rules of the sport, then you know what you can and can't do, how far you can take things and you can innovate.

Mental Toughness:

Mental toughness can get you out of tough situations and helps you to keep focused. Signs of mental toughness are:

* Able to get back up after being physically or mentally knocked down.

* Keep persisting when things haven't gone well or right.

* Keep composure and working through when negative remarks and put downs are aimed at you.

* Keep playing right to the end of play.

* Puts bad calls behind them and gets straight back onto the task at hand.

Fitness

Regardless of which sport you play, without being fit for the sport, it doesn't matter how brilliant you are, you'll never compete at a high level. One thing I have noticed is that if you have a natural skill level, you'll have a natural fitness that goes with it. It's almost like a gift for you to use your talents. I've seen so many people squander this gift and never achieve what they are capable of.

Another side of fitness which is ignored is the recovery side. I've seen people go hell for leather all the time, done it myself, and all that eventually happens is that you end up breaking down. Fitness also covers how quickly you can recover between exercises.

Here is a quick explanation for the different areas of fitness.

Stamina:

Can you keep going for the whole game and tournament? Are you able to recover quickly from sprinting?

5 Meter Speed:

How quickly do you move over the first 5 meters, or are you always arriving late?

Strength:

Do you have the strength necessarily to compete in your sport and execute the skills?

Flexibility:

Are you as stiff as a board or are your muscles and joints quite supple?

Agility:

Are you able to move around the field, executing the skills whilst maintaining balance?

That's all the dry ingredients covering the key skills; we'll now cover the wet ingredients which deals with the player attributes required to build your picture.

Wet Ingredients

Without the wet ingredients, it doesn't matter how well you do the rest, it just wont come off as well as it should. You need to implement all three areas to this phase, they being **self discipline, commitment** and **harmony**, to bind your team together.

People and teams that go a long way are self motivated, are extremely self disciplined, are committed to what they want to achieve, and get along in a harmonious way. Harmony is generally left out from most teams, as people are working to their own self interests or playing the popularity game or they just don't work at harmony in their own life.

Self Discipline

There is two ways to enforce self discipline. The first way is by having rules and regulations or players can cultivate their own self discipline and this is achieved if players are self motivated and they will do what they need to do to achieve.

Practice Attendance:

Without regular attendance and on time attendance, all good intentions and goals go out the window unless you are extremely skillful, have a natural fitness and play in a low level competition.

Repetition of Skills and drills at practice:

This is an excellent way to develop your skills and develop your self discipline. By repetition, you will also develop the neural pathways and muscle memory to develop the skills into the subconscious.

When you can start executing the basics and skills subconsciously, then by not having to consciously think about them, you can start the scanning process while you're executing the skill, there by you start creating more time for yourself on the field, and also begin to manipulate the opposition to get them to go where you want them to be.

Practice in own time:

Players who are committed and self disciplined want to improve by practicing in their own time. What you are doing at practice is really gelling, moulding and fine tuning, especially if you are getting ready for a tournament.

Commitment

If players are not going to be there for the team, you're not going to go very far.

To the Team:

When players are required to be with the team, are they there? They maybe there physically and their mind is some where else. Are they always turning up late, missing practices? Players not practicing during their own time? Do they want to be there or are they there by default.

To keep improving:

Basically between what one says and actually does. (Between words and deeds) I have had people go really enthusiastically, *"Yeah, yeah, I want to improve, I want to get better, I want to play in the higher team and I want to play at a higher level."*

That's as far as it went. Plenty of intention, but no intent. Subsequently they never hung around long after that.

Harmony

To achieve harmony, you have to put self interests and personal gain to the way side and start working towards the common good and achieving it in a positive fashion.

I've seen people working for the common good but trying to achieve it by antagonizing and working against one another. They may get results in the short term but it doesn't do anything to create harmony in the side.

The more I speak to people, the more harmony comes to the fore. As I'm speaking to people, you can almost see the longing and also the desperation for harmony, but they are not sure how to achieve it because they do not actively work for it in their own life.

Work to team goals:

Is everyone heading in the same direction or are their own goals taking them in a different direction.

Work with others:

Can they work with other people or are they very self indulgent. If so then I suggest they take up an individual sport. **People working towards harmony always find ways to help other people succeed, as well as themselves.**

You can get the situation where you have people who don't like each other, but because they want to achieve the same goals, and they play the same sport they can put aside those differences while they are with the team. It may not be the most ideal situation, but if they are not being disruptive, it can work.

Interacts with people with a positive effect:

They get the best out of people. They do not play the popularity game. Gets on and does the job for the greater good in a positive manner.

Because you try to develop harmony in your team, does not mean there won't be any disagreements or rough bits along the way. If you work to develop harmony in your side, the journey will be a lot of fun and will be over before you realize it.

One of the secrets of being a winning coach is to isolate the key skills and the most effective techniques for executing the skills and practicing them.

We'll now shift onto the second exercise to identify the key skills for your sport and carry on the process of preparing a winning team.

As part of the second exercise, the following is an example of a list of key skills needed for the teams I coach for the sport of field hockey:

Dry ingredients – Basis of Sport

Field Play	*Goal Scoring*	*Defending*
* Body Position	* Feet towards Ball	* Marking
* Hand Positions	* Position in Circle	* Position in circle
* Ball Control	* Low Body Position	* Low Body Position
* Box Hitting	* Aggression	* Aggression
* Upright Trapping	* Scoring Execution	* Clearance Execution
* Pushing the Ball		
* Sweep Hitting		
* Back Tackling		
* Use of Reverse stick to gather the ball		

Skill Level	*Thinking*	*Fitness*
* Hand eye Co ordination	* Game Scenarios	* Stamina
	* Structual Play	* 5 Meter Speed
	* Read the Play	* Agility
	* Communicates	* Flexibility
	On Field	* Strength
	* Knows the Rules	

Wet Ingredients – Binds team together

Self Discipline	*Commitment*	*Harmony*
* Practice Attendance	* To the Team	* To Team Goals
* Repetition of	* Keep Improving	* Work with Others
Skills and Drills		* Interacts with others
		With a positive effect

Now it's your turn, **for the second exercise to identify your ingredients,** write down the key skills you need for your sport.

Dry Ingredients – These form the basis of your sport.

Basics	**Goal scoring**	**Defending**
1:	1:	1:
2:	2:	2:
3:	3:	3:
4:	4:	4:
5:	5:	5:
6:		
7:		
8:		
9:		
10:		

Skill Level (co ordination)

1:
2:

Thinking Abilities

1:
2:
3:
4:
5:

Fitness Components

1:

2:

3:

4:

5:

Wet Ingredients – These bind your team together

Self Discipline

1:

2:

3:

4:

Commitment

1:

2:

Harmony

1:

2:

3:

When you complete this exercise, you will have the ingredients to work with when you are putting together your training program.

You've now got your key skills and player attributes; you need something to follow to be able to combine them together which will enable you to achieve the picture you have developed.

The third step is the recipe.

Step 3
The Recipe

In baking you follow a written recipe that shows how to mix all the ingredients together.

A recipe is nothing more than a method of putting something together.

In baking, you have a list of your ingredients you need. For Example:

190g butter
220g butter, extra for filling
½ cup sugar
3 eggs
100g cooking chocolate
280g cooking chocolate, extra
1 ¼ cups self raising flour
3 tbs baking cocoa
½ cup milk
½ cup cream

Then you follow the written method for putting the ingredients together:

1. Beat 190 g butter and sugar until creamy, beats eggs one at a time. Beat in cooled, melted 100 g cooking chocolate.
2. Fold in sifted flour and baking cocoa alternatively with milk. Spoon mixture into greased 25cm deep round cake pan.
3. Bake in a pre heated 190 degree celcius oven for 45 – 50 minutes until cooked. Remove from pan, cool on wire rack.
4. Melt and cool 80 g of the extra cooking chocolate, combine with cream, beat until thick. Cut cake in half, sandwich cake with chocolate cream.
5. Melt together remaining cooking chocolate and butter, allow to cool, refrigerate until mixture is of spreading consistency. Spread mixture over cake.

It's the same for sport; you take the dry ingredients of the:

Sports basics/key skills

Skill level

Thinking

Fitness

And use a method to combine them to attain the picture you've come up with.

You also use the wet ingredients to bind your team together.

Self discipline

Commitment

Harmony

In baking you use a mixing bowl to combine all you ingredients together.

In sport you use practices to combine all your ingredients.

This area is where the real art of coaching comes in to it and is probably the hardest part of the whole equation.

You can give every one the same aim and set of ingredients and how everything is put together is all slightly different. It all comes down to how each individual works.

That's what makes up the beauty of sport; you'll never end up with exactly the same product because there are so many variables to work with and every team and every season continues to provide new challenges.

Organizing Practices

Let's first look at the alternative and how most people work when it comes to coaching and organizing their practices.

As a coach:

* You do not have a clear picture to what you are trying to achieve on the field.

* You do not have a style of play for your team, except for running round at 100 miles an hour.

* You don't know what type of player you are trying to develop

* You have a bit of an idea of how you want to play on the field

* You've been to coaching clinics and learnt skills for your sport.

Let's see what happens when you organize your practices.

* What are your priorities for practice?

* What skills are you going to focus on?

* What are you going to do at practices to develop your players?

* Do your practices revolve around stopping the opposition or trying to achieve objectives out on the field?

* You've been to coaching clinics, you've been shown some great drills, so you want to give them a go and try them, but what are these drills going to achieve for you?

* Is everything you doing only taking you towards the next game you are playing?

Without a clear picture or aim, you lack a direction in where you are heading and it creates more questions than answers. If you have:

* No idea of the type of game you want to play

* No idea of the style of game you want to play

* No idea of what skills you need

* No idea of what type of player you are trying to develop

* And only a vague idea of how you want to play on the field

How are you going to measure how effective your practices are if you have got nothing to aim for except your next game and hopefully getting a win?

Let's look at organizing practices if you have a clear picture of and:

* Know the type of game you are going to play

* Know the style of game you are going to play

* Know the skills you need

* Know the type of player you are developing

* Know your own coaching method to work your team

All of a sudden with a clear picture to work towards, you have a direction when it comes to organizing your practices. You are able to measure whether what you are trying and doing at practices is moving you towards your aims.

If you have got a picture or aim of what you are building towards, then you know if something is working for or against you and can adjust accordingly.

Here is the Coaching Method I use for a team I coach

* I have got a 1 hour time slot on the hockey turf for the teams practice.

* I have got my teams practice time broken down into 10 – 15 minute time bites, with the last 15 minutes to be used for set piece practice.

* The team I am working with, their techniques for the skill levels and body position need to be worked on. The first 10 minutes of each practice will be allocated for this each week.

* Team fitness training will be done on a separate day to team practices.

* I will be using repetition of skills and drills at practices.

* I will be enforcing the basic techniques of my sport as we complete the various skills and drills at practices.

* The team I am working with, their thinking ability is lacking. I will be asking them two questions at the end of every practice to bring this part of their game up to standard.

* I will be getting the players to identify 2 areas they are deficient in and 1 area they are strong in, for them to improve in their own time.

* I will be working on players goal scoring techniques.

* I will be working on players receiving techniques.

We'll now shift onto the third exercise to carry on preparing a winning team.

For the third exercise, to develop your coaching method, write down how you construct your practices to work your ingredients.

1:

2:

3:

4:

5:

6:

7:

When you have completed this exercise, you will have your method for coaching. If you are coaching a number of sides, depending on their ages and abilities, your methods may vary slightly for each team.

You can now imagine you've mixed all the ingredients together, put the mixture into the cake tin and then serve up the gooey mess to people to eat. I'm sure they wouldn't be very impressed.

Mixing the ingredients on their own isn't enough to produce a cake. You need something to activate your ingredients into the desired result.

In baking it's an oven. In sport it's the coach.

Let's move onto the fourth step to see how you as a person work your team.

Step 4
The Oven

This step is the smallest in the book, though it is the most important. If you attend coaching clinics, this area isn't covered and regardless of all your knowledge, ultimately how you work your players to get the best out of them will determine your results.

It is now time to cook and activate your ingredients into the desired product and what you are aiming for. When baking you use an oven to apply heat to activate the ingredients. In sport, the heat is how the coach interacts with the players to get the best out of them.

To get the best out of players comes down to one thing. That one thing is **Trust**.

Without trust, it doesn't matter how good of a coach you are, players won't be willing to give of themselves fully to the cause of the team.

Trust covers a number of points, some being:

* The ability to keep your word

* Not playing one person against the other

* Consistency of decisions

* In that you know what you are doing

* That you know your stuff

Basically, **if you trust some one you'll do anything for them.**

When baking, you pre heat the oven to the required temperature before you put the mixture in. In coaching, this can equate to your reputation preceding you. One thing to be aware of, not all ovens and coaches are the same and their temperature settings do vary.

As you develop your coaching, are you getting better with age or do you need some repair work done to help improve?

As a coach, to apply heat, you do not have to yell and scream at the players all the time, if at any. You can pick your moment, if need be, and because you haven't let fly very often, it will be much more effective when you do.

If mistakes happen, players know when they have done wrong and if trust has been built then a quiet word can be all that is needed to rectify the situation.

Here is what I am actively looking to do as a coach to get the best out of my teams and to prepare for the games they play.

As a coach I am:

* Actively creating harmony in the side

* Getting players to work for each other

* Getting players to raise their standards

* Getting players to self analyze themselves

* Getting the best out of all players

* Getting the best result possible for the team

* Improving my knowledge of the game

* Continually refining my methods at practices to get results quicker

We'll now shift onto the fourth exercise to carry on preparing a winning team.

For the fourth exercise, as a coach, write down what you do to activate your ingredients and what do you do to get the best out of and develop your players.

1:

2:

3:

4:

5:

6:

7:

8:

When you have completed this exercise and the other three, you will have developed your own philosophy and method for coaching. You will know how you prepare your sides and whether what you are doing is working for you or not.

What you have written down will not be the final say on the way you coach.

These four exercises are a work in progress. As you gain more experience in coaching you will continually be adding to and adjusting the way you do things, therefore keep reviewing these exercises, to improve what you have written down, as you develop into a better coach.

Success isn't always in the playing numbers

It's in the attitude and how you train them

The Results

If you've followed the steps for baking I've outlined and applied them to your sports team, you should have got a result you were after.

As with baking, the proof is with the final product. Did you fluke it and your cake came out alright once or can you keep producing the final product over and over again with any team you take?

Did you ice the cake and put the decorations on, eg: come first.

Coming first is equivalent to putting those small finishing touches on which helps lift the cake out of the pack.

If you didn't get the desired results you were after, you will have to look at the appropriate parts and adjust them until you achieved your desired results. To get to your desired results you may have to adjust either:

* **The Playing Aim or Picture**

* **The Ingredients**

* **The Recipe**

* **The Oven**

When baking a cake, you can ditch it if it didn't come out right and immediately start again in the same day.

With sport the adjustment process is a lot slower as the build up for games, tournaments and finals is stretched over a period of time.

This is why **to become a really good and effective coach is a process which can take a number of years.** The reason being is you have more ingredients and variables to work with and you are dealing with people.

*Expand your knowledge
and see if you still come
to the same conclusion*

Summary

What I have done with the contents of this book, is to take the complicated and confusing information that surrounds coaching, taken it apart and reassembled it in an easy to understand format and language so people can apply it to their own situation and gain winning results without knowing all the deep theory behind it. For example, you don't need to be a mechanic to know how to drive a car.

As with anything, it is up to you as a coach to put the information into action, for without action nothing will happen.

If you think I've simplified the coaching process too much, Albert Einstein simplified things best when he described his theory of relativity as:

$$E=MC2$$

By also completing the exercises I have included, it will make you examine and clarify what you are doing, for if you can not write down and **explain to yourself what you want to achieve on the field, the key skills and attributes needed to achieve it and how you are going to make it happen via your coaching methods**, for if you do not know, how are your players going to know.

This is what the process is about, for the more you can clarify to yourself, the better you can explain it and put it to your players in a language they can understand and use, and if you are working with age group players, then be able to explain it to their parents, legal guardians or care givers if required.

The next four pages, starting with the aim and picture, is a practical example of how you can put all of the previous information into use. It is all the information I've taken from my experiences as a coach to come up with my aim, picture, ingredients, method and how I work as a coach to develop and get the best out of the players and sides that I take to put them on the path to success.

If you know the process
to be successful

Then you can train
for Success

The Aim and Picture

Playing aim: Is to play the best type of hockey we can

* We are playing a flowing game, with accurate passing through the midfield. (Passing game between the 25's) If I haven't got the ball I am making myself available for passes.

* We are moving the ball across the field away from congestion, especially after gaining a turnover and we have the ability to switch the play at any time.

* We are organized in defence and attack and there is plenty of communication on the field in letting each other know what is happening, by either directing traffic or calling for the ball.

* We are creating many goal scoring opportunities during the game which we put away efficiently either by ourselves or with the use of our team mates, by using the correct techniques inside the circle.

* We are taking our penalties quick and when defending penalties, are setting up quicker than the opposition is taking theirs.

* We are creating width and space when we have the ball and creating congestion when the opposition has the ball.

* We are showing desperation in defence and aggression in attack to get the ball, for the whole game.

* We are working as a unit when we are on the field, playing structurally in both attack and defence.

* We are skillful players who are adept at executing the basics of field hockey with the correct techniques, to a high standard.

* We are game smart and mentally tough enough to combat and react to any situation that is occurring on the field.

* We take pride in the way we play and practice and act in the manner befitting that of a quality sports person.

The Ingredients

Key Skills Needed

Dry ingredients – Basis of Sport

Field Play	*Goal Scoring*	*Defending*
* Body Position	* Feet towards Ball	* Marking
* Hand Positions	* Position in Circle	* Position in circle
* Ball Control	* Low Body Position	* Low Body Position
* Box Hitting	* Aggression	* Aggression
* Upright Trapping	* Scoring Execution	* Clearance Execution
* Pushing the Ball		
* Sweep Hitting		
* Back Tackling		
* Use of Reverse stick to gather the ball		

Skill Level	*Thinking*	*Fitness*
* Hand eye Co ordination	* Game Scenarios	* Stamina
	* Structual Play	* 5 Meter Speed
	* Read the Play	* Agility
	* Communicates On Field	* Flexibility
	* Knows the Rules	* Strength

Wet Ingredients – Binds team together

Self Discipline	*Commitment*	*Harmony*
* Practice Attendance	* To the Team	* To Team Goals
* Repetition of Skills and Drills	* Keep Improving	* Work with Others
		* Interacts with others With a positive effect

The Recipe

Coaching Method

* I have got a 1 hour time slot on the hockey turf for the teams practice.

* I have got my team practice times broken down into 10 – 15 minute time bites, with the last 15 minutes to be used for set pieces.

* The team I am working with, their techniques for the skill levels and body position need to be worked on. The first 10 minutes of each practice will be allocated for this every week.

* Team fitness training will be done on a separate day to team practices.

* I will be using repetition of skills and drills at practices.

* I will be enforcing the basic techniques of my sport as we complete the various skills and drills at practices.

* The team I am working with, their thinking ability is lacking. I will be asking them two questions at the end of every practice to bring this part of their game up to standard.

* I will be getting the players to identify 2 areas they are deficient in and 1 area they are strong in, for them to improve in their own time.

* I will be working on players goal scoring techniques.

* I will be working on players receiving techniques.

The Heat Source

As a coach I am actively:

* Creating harmony in the side

* Getting players to work for each other

* Getting the players to raise their standards

* Getting the players to self analyses themselves

* Getting the best out of all players

* Getting the best result possible for the team

* Improving my knowledge of the game

* Continually refine my methods at practices to get results quicker

If you haven't done the exercises to develop your playing philosophy and coaching method, I've grouped them together in the following pages.

By taking the time to complete them, you will gain a better understanding of how you work. **By having a better understanding of how you work, then you'll be able to work a lot more efficient and smarter and gain better results.**

It is time to start the process of preparing a winning team. Begin by writing down your playing aim and then move onto the four exercises.

My playing aim for the teams I coach is …….

For the first exercise, to build your picture, write down what an ideal game would be like for your sport based on your playing aim.

Name the type of game you would like to play:

Name the style of game that you would like to play through the midfield:

Name the type of player you would like to develop:

What attributes do the best players in your sport display?

1:

2:

3:

4:

5:

6:

7:

Identify how you would want to play on the field, what would be your ideal game:

1:

2:

3:

4:

5:

6:

7:

8:

9:

10:

When you have completed this exercise, you will have a picture of what you are working towards.

For the second exercise to identify your ingredients, write down the key skills you need for your sport.

Dry Ingredients – They form the basis of your sport.

Basics	Goal scoring	Defending
1:	1:	1:
2:	2:	2:
3:	3:	3:
4:	4:	4:
5:	5:	5:
6:		
7:		
8:		
9:		
10:		

Skill Level (co ordination)

1:

2:

Thinking Abilities

1:
2:
3:
4:
5:

Fitness Components

1:
2:
3:
4:
5:

Wet Ingredients – They bind your team together

Self Discipline

1:
2:
3:
4:

Commitment

1:
2:

Harmony

1:
2:
3:

When you complete this exercise, you will have the ingredients to work with when you are putting together your training program.

You worked out your key skills and player attributes, how do you present it to your players?

What I've used successfully, is to set out all of the skills required on a spread sheet, rate each one on a scale of 1 to 5, assigned a different colour for each number. On the spread sheet you can block in the colours and by having the colours, it makes it more visual. I've also worked out a standard I'm aiming for and have the persons score beside the standard. When you do update it periodically, you can instantly see if the players are improving or not and so can they.

You also have to explain to the players not to look at is as a negative, there is no pass mark. It is designed as a help tool to improve them at their sport.

An example of what I have used is on the following pages.

Player Checklist – Hockey Team

Name: **Fiona Whoever**
Position on field: **Back**

Basics:	Aim For	16/08/06	15/10/08	23/09/09
Body Position	5	2	4	5
Hand Position	5	2	4	5
Ball Control	4	3	4	4
Box Hitting	4	2	3	4
Upright Trapping	5	2	4	5
Pushing Ball	4	2	4	4
Sweep Hitting	4	3	4	4
Back Tackling	5	2	4	4
Use of Reverse stick	5	2	4	4

Goal Scoring:

Feet towards Ball	**5**	3	3	3
Position in circle	**4**	3	3	3
Low body position	**5**	3	3	3
Aggression to ball	**5**	3	3	3
Scoring Execution	**4**	3	3	3

Defence in circle:

Marking	**5**	2	4	5
Position in circle	**5**	3	4	5
Low Body position	**5**	2	5	5
Aggression to ball	**5**	3	5	5
Clearance execution	**4**	3	3	4

Skill:

Handeye Co ordination	**4**	3	3	4

Thinking Ability:

Game scenarios	**4**	2	5	5
Structual Play	**5**	2	5	5
Read the play	**5**	3	5	5
Communicates Onfield	**5**	3	5	5
Knows game rules	**4**	3	3	4

Fitness:

Stamina	**4**	2	2	3

5 meter speed	**4**	2	3	3
Agility	**3**	2	2	3
Flexibility	**3**	2	2	3

Self Discipline:

Practice attendance	**5**	5	5	5
Repetition of skills & drills	**5**	5	5	5

Commitment:

To team	**5**	5	5	5
To keep improving	**5**	5	5	5

Harmony:

Work to team goals	**5**	5	5	5
Work with others	**5**	5	5	5
Interacts with a positive effect	**5**	5	5	5

Total Score	164	107	141	153
Out of	<u>180</u>	<u>180</u>	<u>180</u>	<u>180</u>
Average	4.55	2.97	3.91	4.25

Points awarded as

1	2	3	4	5
Poor	**Work on**	**Sufficient**	**Good**	**Excellent**

For the third exercise to develop your coaching method, write down how you construct your practices to work your ingredients.

1:

2:

3:

4:

5:

6:

7:

When you have completed this exercise, you will have your method for coaching.

If you are coaching a number of sides, depending on their ages and abilities, your methods may vary slightly for each team.

For the fourth exercise, as a coach, write down what you do to activate your ingredients and what do you do to get the best out of and develop your players.

1:

2:

3:

4:

5:

6:

7:

8:

When you have completed this exercise, you will know how you prepare your sides and whether what you are doing is working for you or not. By also completing these exercises you will gain a great advantage over someone who does not, as you will know exactly what you are doing in making your teams successful. For **if you know the process to be successful, then you can train for success.**

If you can't explain to yourself what you're trying to achieve and how you're going to achieve it

How can you explain it to your players?

In reality, it doesn't matter what you do in life, whether it's baking a cake, coaching a sports team or anything else you undertake, if:

You've got your picture

Got your ingredients

Followed your recipe

Your ovens working properly

You can only succeed in getting the results you are after, or better.

Who would have thought that baking a cake and coaching a sports team would have so much in common?

Principles are a Constant.

*Rules and Regulations
can be changed to suit.*

Game Experience

If you can avoid prejudices

A good idea is a good idea

Regardless of the source

A fair proportion of sport is about how you play the game in your head and then having the skill set to be able to execute the plan on the field.

This section of the book is to help you understand different nuances of sport which can take years of playing and coaching to accumulate. You could be watching or playing tennis, hockey, football, rugby, boxing or tiddly winks. It doesn't matter. The ebbs and flows of the game are the same, for sport is all played by humans. The principles will be the same, though the application for each sport will be different.

Though sport appears random, if you watch enough and analyze what is happening, you can see the same patterns and situations occurring, especially the type and style of games played and how people are reacting on the field. **If you can find these patterns and situations for your sport, you will become a more effective coach.** Again it's building that picture of what you want and being able to recognize patterns and situations on the field, and then having the skill set to be able to rectify and control what is happening.

As a coach, when I am standing on the side line, I am taking in what is happening on the field and comparing it to the information and experiences I have stored in my memory, e.g. where are people standing on the field or who is moving where? If you know what you're looking for or can recognize situations happening and have the instant answers, then you can take quicker steps to rectify it, though some situations can not be rectified during a game and have to be worked on during practices.

While watching a game you can go, this is starting to happen, if the players do this, it will get them out of the situation, if they don't do anything or react in a certain way, the game will get away from them. It can be as simple as that. We've all seen it as well, something goes against a player, they maybe targeted by the opposition, or get some bad calls by the officials, they react, get carded and then lose their composure and then are ineffective for the rest of the game and then their team can go on to lose a game they should have won.

If you want to accumulate experience quicker, coach more teams, watch more sport, ask more questions and apply what you learn. **Preparation and then application is a key to success in sport.**

Mindset

If you want to achieve or do any thing, you have to have the right mind set that enables you to accomplish it.

End of story.

If you want to you can, if you don't you wont.

It doesn't matter how much the coach can cajole the players into action, if the players head space isn't in the right frame of mind, they won't perform, especially when it matters, unless their backs happen to be against the wall and they have to do some thing to save face and their reputation.

This is where the coaching process is so important and what you do and say at practices really comes to the fore.

What people generally don't realize is that practices aren't just about getting players skills right for the games, it's also about working on their head space and getting them prepared for action so when the time comes, the players actually motivate themselves. Then all it can take from the coaches is a few quite and key words in the right place and to the right people.

Occasionally you may have to let rip to get the players going. Let this be the rare exception rather than the rule. You want to get the players to play well because they want to, not because they have to.

If you yell at your players too much they eventually tune out to you.

Dangers of a 2 goal lead

As a coach or player, always be aware of the 2 goal lead or bad comfort zone syndrome in what ever sport you play.

A 2 goal lead is more dangerous than only leading by a single goal for the reason that when you are leading by one goal your players are still generally focused and concentrating because of the closeness of the score.

When the score is increased to a two goal lead, subconsciously the players can think *"we've done all the hard work and for the opposition to win they have to score three goals"*. This sort of thinking is compounded if your team has had a lot of scoring chances but they haven't converted that pressure into points.

If your players do drop in intensity, it can be hard to get them going again, especially if they do not recognize it themselves.

To help keep your players focused, you have to keep them striving for that third goal. This is always hard against teams of similar ability to you because every time you score a goal that option will be closed to you for their defense will make sure you will not score from that option again.

Another area to be aware of is if your team has a three goal lead, or some similar lead, depending on the sport played, and your players relax just before the half time break and the opposition score. Even though your team still has a two goal lead, more concern is that the momentum of the game has shifted back to the opposition and your team is back to the above two goal lead.

Another killer with the same effect as above is scoring in the first minute of play, (obviously not for basketball or netball of which both are high scoring games). Regardless of how your players react, again they can subconsciously think, *"That was easy, this is going to be a cake walk"* and they can drop the intensity and allow the opposition back into the game. Conversely the opposition think, *"We allowed them to score to easily, we'd better harden up and put an effort in"* and they generally do.

I learnt the lesson of the 2 goal lead many years ago when I was at an age group tournament as a 12 year old. There were 3 games we were up by 2 goals and ended up losing 3 – 2. Wish our coaches had known about it back then.

In a recent final, the team I was coaching was down 2 nil and when approaching half time, we scored just before the blow of the whistle. The game continued in the second half and we were still down 1 goal with 17 seconds to go, when we were awarded a corner which we scored from. The game went to extra time and then went to strokes, which we won and took home the trophy.

All the time now I see sides get out to a 2 goal lead and then go onto lose. A lot of it is to be aware and keep striving for that 3rd goal and do not give the opposition a sniff of a chance to get back into the game. If you give them a sniff, they will lift their effort, and you'll just make your job that much harder. That's why you've got to keep the pressure on them.

Startled rabbit Syndrome

In field hockey and other related ball sports, we've all seen it.

The ball is delivered to your forwards, whether on your defensive 25 or halfway and they take off with the ball at 100mph, hence the startled rabbit.

They beat one player, beat two and if lucky, beat a third player, get near the opposition 25, get tackled, your teams' precious possession is turned over and there is a big gap back to your support players.

The opposition then turns around and does exactly the same. This provides for a frenetic game, and possibly an exciting game. This can be deceiving as there is a lot happening but not a lot being achieved.

The above happens so often, from primary grades right through to internationals that it appears the natural and normal way to play.

Would it not be better to build your play with structure, intelligent decision making and controlled team work up to the opposition 25, and then launch your attacks?

 If the ball is turned over from the above, then your support players will be there in numbers to get the ball back.

To start to change this startled rabbit syndrome, what is required is a big shift in mental thought.

The front strike forwards, regardless of the numbers, have to consider themselves as part of the midfield, albeit the top parts, and actively play a passing game through the midfield until they reach near the opposition 25.

This does not preclude the strikers from being forwards at any opportunity. What it does allow for is better controlled possession of the ball for better use at more opportune moments.

Now that you can recognize it, the question to consider is this, how do you go from the startled rabbit syndrome to playing a controlled possession game?

The answer is fairly straight forward.

Players have to:

Have the **mind set** that they want to play a passing game through the midfield

The **self discipline** to be able to execute it

And **provide movement off the ball** to put them selves in a position to receive the ball.

If players do not receive the ball from a pass, then they have to move into another position to make them selves available.

Again it sounds very straight forward. The difficulty is in getting the players to do the same actions over and over again, and not to be disappointed if they do not receive the ball. For a player moving in one direction, may open up a space for the ball to go in another direction.

Just because you haven't got the ball doesn't mean you're not influencing the game.

Captaincy

Captaincy, what does it really entail?

I know people get hooked in to the prestige of it all, got to lead from the front, got to be the example for everyone, follow me mentality.

Of course you get the other side of captaincy, the petty politics, the maneuvering and manipulation, the power and popularity games.

If we take the emotion out of captaincy, what do they actually do?

The best description I've heard is some one who calls the toss and decides which way to go.

That maybe a bit simplistic, but it pretty well sums it up. I've never placed too much importance on captaincy; to me it's just a job and a role to do. I got sick of people wanting the captaincy one year because it was the perceived prestigious position within the team and because I'm not into popularity games, I decided to have no captain in the side, and instead I created roles for two people.

One person was to be responsible for looking after the administration duties for the team on the field, such as:

* Calling the toss

* Letting the umpires know whether we want the ball or which way we will go

* Speak and communicate with umpires if needed

* Cheers at the start and finish of a game

Because they were looking after the administration duties I put their name down as captain on the card and in the tournament program. As I explained, **it is purely for the benefit of the umpires and officials,** so they know who to deal with when sorting through the on field administration duties.

The other person was to be responsible for and looking after:

* The warm-ups

* The warm downs

As well as

* Provide inspiration on the field

* And be responsible for the harmony in the side and everyone working well together at all times.

By doing this it solved a lot of problems because the people involved knew what was being asked of them and the role they were to play and everyone else was aware of what was being asked of both people.

The captaincy can be a prestigious role and it comes with certain responsibilities, I think we can forget what these are and start to attach to much emotion and baggage to captaincy, at the expense of doing the job and without knowing the role that they play.

Tournaments

Tournaments are great. You get to find out real quick whether what you are doing is working or not and can expose your short comings very quickly.

I've been involved in tournaments where I've been struggling for survival and in other tournaments where I'm going for the top prize.

I've been in the situation where my team is playing a game to put them through to the top 8 at a national tournament and by the end of the game, been knocked out of the top 16 and then playing for their survival to stay in that grade the next year.

I've been in the situation where I've had to use my best players most of the time during pool play just to try and win games, and I've been in the situation where I've been able to rotate players around and use my second tier players more in pool play so I can keep my top players rested for the business end of tournaments.

I've been involved in penalty shoot outs (which most coaches hate, I love them) in quarter finals, semis and finals.

The following is some tips I've picked up which will prove of benefit to you.

* The first pool game of tournament is like a semi final, every one wants to win it to get off to a good start. The intensity of the game is normally quite high because it's the first game, and with the combinations of nerves, excitement, expectations and everyone's rearing to go. Unlike a semi final, if you do lose your opener, you do get another chance.

* If you are a top side, during pool play, at some stage you will have a game against a lesser side where you will struggle to win it or only come away with a draw, and it will be a battle right through to the end.

That's just the nature of tournament.

When you get to the business end of tournaments, the:

* **Quarter finals** can be harder to win than a semi final. The reason being, it's every ones chance to make the top four. If that's not a good enough reason for everyone to play well, you shouldn't be there.

* **Semi finals**, this is the time mental toughness starts to come to the fore. After a week or month long tournament, consisting of pool play and quarters, have you got enough fuel left in the tank to perform, both physically and mentally. If both teams have, you're in for a good game. If one team hasn't, it could be a cake walk.

* **Finals**, maintain the focus, work the process, create the pressure, have the right mind set, be strong and game smart.

Working the process is everything that you've been doing that goes into creating the successful game you've been playing. Focus on the process, not the win.

What happens if the games are all tied up, done extra time (if played), it goes into penalty shoot outs. How do you cope? A lot don't.

There's an art to penalty shoot outs and it's quite simple.

* Practice them in training.

On the day:

* As a coach, remain calm and detached, not for your self, but for your players.

* Have your order worked out in advance.

* It's not how well your first two go, it's your third, fourth and fifth takers. (An order I've used successfully is 2, 1, 5, 4, and 3. In sudden death the order naturally becomes 1, 2, 3, 4 and 5.)

* Tell your players to picture where they're going to put it and put it there. (Work on the process, not the result)

* Expect to win penalty shoot outs.

* Be grateful when you do.

If the penalty shoot out does not go your way, about the only thing you can say is, that's tournaments for you.

You can actually play really well for a whole tournament, lose a crucial game and suddenly you are playing in the wrong half of the table. Consequently you can be struggling for most of the tournament, luckily you have a relatively easy pool, win the right crucial games and you can be into a final before you even know it. That's tournaments.

I've had a tournament, where my team was down 3 – 1 in the first pool game with 15 minutes to go. We had scored early on in the game and as the half progressed my team started to drift off the intensity, though we still led 1 nil at the break. The opposition scored immediately after the break, and then another 2 quick goals to give them a two goal lead. I made a couple of changes, thankfully the girls hit the turbo boost, gained the momentum and scored three quick goals in 10 minutes and walked away with a win they shouldn't have had, but we took the win. The girls went onto win the rest of their games to finish top of the pool.

The Quarter final ended in a 2 all draw. Normally we'd beat this side by 1 to 2 goals, so we had to go into strokes. Won that one 4 – 3.

The Semi final ended in a nil all draw. Strokes were tied up 4 all after the first 5, so it was into sudden death. The girls got their first two in, the oppositions 2nd one hit the post, and we progressed to the final.

We didn't take out the top prize. That's tournaments for you.

The biggest thing about tournaments is not to lose heart. Re evaluate, and then move on.

One thing to remember:

The best teams do not always win tournaments.
The best prepared teams do.

How umpires can affect a game

Quite simply **there are six things an umpire or umpires can do to influence a game for the negative.**

* **They can slow the game down** by insisting the ball is taken exactly from the spot of the infringement, even if that is only a movement of one meter of the ball and also waiting until the penalty is taken before deciding it needs to go back to the mark where the infringement occurred.

* **50 – 50 decisions tend to keep going in the favour of 1 team** over the other, whether intentional or not

* **Not playing advantage** in field play for the attacking side but especially around the goal scoring area by blowing the whistle on the first instance of an infringement which kills any momentum being created by the attack.

* **Not using arm signals or verbal cues** to indicate they are playing advantage.

* If more than one official is used for a game, they **do not work together as a team.**

* **Not looking for negative, off the ball play.**

By combining some or all six together an umpire can create a situation by ham stringing one side in which he creates an artificial close game.

This is negative umpiring because it doesn't allow the players to get the best out of themselves and it actually holds players back. Their rate of improvement is being retarded because they lose confidence in what they can do.

If umpires are umpiring negatively, it makes for a horrible game for spectators to watch. This is because of the stop start nature of the game, due to the lack of flow and is generally quite frustrating for players to participate in.

Game Scenarios

The following is a list of real life game scenarios for field hockey, some happen all the time, some only happen occasionally. Most may not even apply to your sport, though they will give you an idea of what you can come up with.

Halves/Backs - Opposition is playing high forwards. How do you combat it? What might you do?

Forwards – You get on the field and discover the opposition has decided to mark you for the whole game, what are you going to do to combat this?

Halves/Backs – You are under pressure, having trouble passing ball out of own 25. What might you do to release the pressure that is building up?

Forwards – Continually turning over possession before half way. What might you do to rectify this?

Halves/Backs – 1 min to go, 1 all, penalty outside defending circle. How do you defend and not concede a Penalty Corner or goal?

Forwards - 1 min to go, 1 all, penalty outside attacking circle. Need a Penalty Corner, how might you achieve one?

Halves/Backs – Opposition Back gets ball, sizes up their options and starts dribbling and keeps dribbling. Who is going to make the first tackle?

Forwards – Opposition half is dribbling with the ball, who is going to make the tackle? How would you stop the half from dribbling initially?

Back and a rounds – How do you make back and a rounds happen as halves and backs? What are the forwards, especially the wings, doing when the ball is going back and around?

Your team is having a bad day on the field. How would you recognize the team is having a bad game? What might you do to rectify it?

As a team you've played an excellent first half. You're 2 – 1 up. What are you going to make sure you play the second half as well, if not better?

You're playing a team which is just as strong as yourself. You've scored 2 quick goals in the first 10 minutes of the game. What are you going to do to make sure you keep the momentum going?

Opposition playing high forwards, especially wings. Our halves are marking wings. We still need to give an outlet pass. How are we going to achieve it?

We've played very well, been attacking plenty, and then we start getting carved up through the middle of the field. Why might this be starting to happen? (Think Playing Structure)

Inners / Halves - The ball is not on your side of the field.

Questions to ask yourself - Am I on the right angle from the ball to prevent it from getting to the wing? Am I in the right channel for my defensive role?

How would we lineup at the start of the game, or after a goal has been scored:

They've got the ball?
We've got the ball?

Opposition goal keeper is saving all your shots at goal. How are you going to beat them?

You've had plenty of attack for three quarters of the game, and have had plenty of goal scoring chances. Scored at best 1 goal, or worse no goals. What are you going to do?

You are getting hit round the back of the legs or sticks in your ribs, what are you going to say or do to the people concerned?

The water turf is bouncy, how are you going to get the ball through the midfield a lot smoother?

Inners – The ball isn't on your side of the field, the inner you are marking is playing wide. Will you go out wide to mark them or play your structural position?

Halves – The ball isn't on your side of the field, the wing you are marking has dropped back very deep. Are you going to go forward to mark them or remain in your structural position?

What effect may these two scenarios, with the opposition inner playing wide and the opposition wing falling back deep, have on the playing structure?

The opposition you are playing has got strong:

Wingers

How are you going to counteract them?

Or strong

Inners

Or strong

Halves

Or strong

Backs

Or strong

Front 3

Or strong

Inners and Centre Forward

Or strong

Inside right and Right wing

Or

Any other Combination of positions on the field

Coaching is about problem solving. The more game scenarios you come up with for your sport and solve them ahead of playing, the fewer surprises you will have at game time.

That's the coaching side covered and **the more pieces of the overall philosophy you use the better results you'll get.** We'll now move onto the principles to follow for developing a winning organisation.

One thing to remember above all else, it doesn't matter how good of a coach, player, umpire, administrator or organisation you are, **you can always get better and improve upon what you've got and done.**

In Summary, the people who go on to become winning coaches and prepare winning teams have:

* **A playing aim and an ideal picture of the way their sport is to be played**

* **A list of key skills and their techniques and practice them**

* **Get the best out of their players**

* **Develop a brain for their sport**

* **Have a recipe or method for putting it all together**

And they aim towards the following three things:

Type of game to play:

A Positive Flowing game.

The style of game they play through the midfield:

A Controlled Short Passing game.

The types of player they develop are:

Class Skillful Thinking Players.

And have an accurate description for the way they want their team to play on the field.

Regardless of how good you are, without a desire to improve, and a willingness to practice, you'll never be the best you can be.

Part 2

Grow a Winning Organization

Building
The
Flower Bed

No light shines dimmer

than in the

darkness of ignorance

The Flower Garden

When developing a sporting organisation, you have to look at the bigger picture. Too many people get voted into positions and only look at it from where they are operating from. They develop blinkers and then think their role is the most important. In reality, they are a cog in the wheel regardless of whether they are the president, CEO or coach. Once a person starts dealing in their own self importance, or holding onto positions because they like the power or control associated with it, then they begin the process of holding back or pulling down an organisation. To be truly successful everybody has to work as one by following sound principles, guidelines and aims.

To understand the path to success, you can compare a sporting organisation to a flower garden.

The flower garden and the sporting organisation are the shell or structure which contains everything.

Into the flower garden, you put the seeds that you want to grow. Here you have a conscious choice, you can let any old seeds grow in the flower garden or you can go, we would like to grow this type of flower and plant the seeds and then put everything to work towards what you have planted. If you are not aware of what you plant, you may end up with a paddock full of weeds.

Seeds = Aims

It's the same with any sporting organisation, with the aims of the organisation being the equivalent of the seeds for the flower garden. Again you have a conscious choice when choosing or adopting specific aims when it comes to all parts of the organisation. **You can adopt the aims you want and nurture and grow them or just let any thing grow and work against each other.**

Some sporting organisations have little concerns about aims, especially for what happens on the playing field, because they are not aware of or do not see the importance of. When you are gardening, a seed is only a small thing when you plant it. The size of the seed has no correlation to the size of the final product.

It's the same with aims. They may seem small and insignificant to most, because they do not understand the relationship between the aim, the process to achieve the aim and the final product.

Soil = Administration

In a flower garden, the seeds take hold in the soil. If you leave the seed out of the soil, it's not going to grow.

It's the same with a sporting organisation; the aims have to take hold within the administration to be able to grow. If the people within the administration do not adopt and give backing for any aims and do not have any structures in place, then it doesn't matter how good the people below are, they will never bloom to their potential.

Water, food and sun = Umpires, players and coaches

To make a seed grow into a flower once it is planted in the garden; it requires three things, they being, water, food and the sun all working together.

If you do not put a seed into the flower bed, it doesn't matter how hard the water, food and sun works, not much will happen.

Conversely, if you do plant a seed, regardless of how good that seed is, and you do not provide water, food or sun to it, the plant will initially start growing but will eventually wither and die.

The water, food and sun for an organisation are your umpires, players and coaches.

All three are important to the growing process. If two are actively working for the process and one is not, it can kill it. If all three aren't working for the process, be happy playing at low levels

Therefore, if the administration, coaches, umpires and players aren't harmoniously working towards the same aims, especially for what happens on the field, then an organisation and everyone involved will never reach the success at a high level they deserve or desire.

Principles for an Organisation
To Attain Success on the Sports Field

Administration

The Administration has got three areas to oversee, they being:

On Field
Finances/Funding
Facilities

Of these, on field is first on the list, there is no point in having first rate facilities, with a third rate competition. Once you get the on field aim in place, then the administration can focus more on the finances and facilities because they are always changing and upgrading.

Most organisations generally only deal with finances and facilities and are generally fighting fires and end up being so occupied in these two areas to see the importance of looking after the on field activities.

For an organisation to succeed on the field it needs to have a playing aim in place so they can have the umpires, coaches and players all working to the same aim and agenda. If you want your organisation to be the best on the field, then the aim has to be for a flowing game.

Some guidelines for administration

* To administrate the game in such a way to make sure that the activities on the field comply with the chosen playing aim and to assist umpires, coaches and players to align themselves with their principles and guidelines for being successful on the field.

* Find ways to achieve the organisations aims by devising sound guidelines and principles to move forward and keep improving.

* To solve any issues which arise with dialogue, common sense and personal abuse kept out of it.

* To foster and develop the sport in the area and create a positive environment for people to learn and develop off each other.

Umpires

If the organisation does not have a playing aim for the type of game to be played on the field, they will get a lot of inconsistency when it comes to umpiring as the organisation is open to too many personal agendas because every one is not actively working towards the same aim, therefore, playing standards are kept low regardless of all the other good work which is being done off the field.

Principles for umpiring a flowing and open game

* Look at the players, not only at the ball

* Look for contact and interference when ball is not on your side of the field

* Keep the game flowing – Apply advantage rule

* Show you are playing advantage by using appropriate hand signals

* Penalties do not need to be taken from the exact spot where the infringement occurred. Can be taken up to 3 to 5 meters away from where the infringement occurred.

* Be consistent with decisions

* Use your whistle properly

* Always use precise hand signals

* Good field position is paramount

With umpiring, the rules of sport do and will continue to change but the principles for achieving a flowing and open game will always remain the same.

Coaches

Winning coaches focus on the following 5 areas:

* Work to and from a philosophy for the type of game and the style of game they want to see played.

* Work on the key skills of the game.

* Works to get the best out of all players.

* Continually work at raising players' match smarts and skill level.

* Have a method or a recipe for putting it all together.

Winning coaches also combine the five areas they focus on, with the four areas that most sports are broken down into, which are:

* Playing structure

* Field play

* Scoring

* Skills

Winning coaches combine the above 9 areas plus the 4 areas that players work on, within their practice structure.

If coaches apply the above then they will set themselves onto the path for becoming master coaches.

A master coach is someone who works to an aim, who does the simple things well, time and time again and has spent their years learning the skills, knowledge and wisdom that enable them to do it.

This is why your best and successful coaches never really occur until later on in their life.

Players

There are four areas successful players work on:

* Self Discipline

* Their Skill Base

* Execution of Key Skills Under Pressure

* Game Smarts

When all four of Administration, Umpires, Coaches and Players work their principles and guidelines, then there is no limitation to what an organization could achieve.

If one or more of the four moves away from their principles and guidelines, then that will begin the downward slide for an organization, away from success.

Success Formulae

Talent + Work Ethic + Self Discipline+ Mental Maturity + Years of Practice

= Success and Achievement at a high level

The following guidelines are for developing and maintaining a successful organization. The more of these an organisation can tick off the more successful they will become.

* Have aims, these provide focus and direction

* Pass on knowledge gained

* Develop structures and systems for operations

* Develop and implement systems and structures for expansion before expanding

* Build what you do on common sense and sound principals

* Have defined pathways

* Be prepared to innovate

* Be prepared to go against the normal ways of doing things

* Write what you do down

* Work on the principal of continual development

* Eliminate petty politics and empire building

* Work for the greater good

* Work on the principal of there must be a better way of doing things

* When you leave an organization it should be in better state than when you arrived

* Look after and nurture people who are special or who have special talents

* Put time and effort into developing everybody

* Remember where you came from

* Success should never be taken for granted

* Have plenty of informal discussions

* Ask questions

* If you don't know the answer to a question, seek to find

* Develop the ability to listen

There you have it. I been involved in sporting organisations where everybody had been working to their own agendas, where **the administrations** most pressing concern were the facilities and funding and what happens on the field was a very distant third, subsequently there was no driving aim for every body to work towards. Nothing was ever discussed unless it was at a meeting or a forum. Sometimes these meetings and forums would continue for up to 3 hours, with many a time nothing being resolved.

The umpires had been working to their own drum beat and not actively been going out to officiate for a flowing and open game. You wouldn't know what you were going to get from game to game and some times even from half to half.

Most of **the players** weren't worried about getting better and their only concern was about getting a win that week.

Few of **the coaches** even wanted to talk about coaching. Even fewer wanted to go to coaching clinics. There was no coaching structure to actively develop coaches.

There was also an us verses them attitude, though not spoken about, was definitely there.

There was much more going on than the above, which created an environment, where mediocrity was the norm. The end result was, at national level we tended to get an occasionally good result, but were mainly in the mid to bottom part of the table, the worse bit was the organisation couldn't work out why. **If only they had an on field aim, put egos aside and began talking and working together.**

Based on everything we've covered, here are seven questions an organisation needs to ask of them selves if they want to go on to become a winning organisation. The more questions you can answer yes to and explain your yes answers, the more successful you will become on the field.

As an Organisation:

* **Do we want to be successful on the sports field?**

* **Do we have a playing aim for the type of game that will ultimately allow us to be successful on the playing field?**

* **Is our administration following and implementing sound principles and guidelines that will allow us to be successful on the playing field?**

* **Are our umpires following the principles and guidelines for blowing the type of game that will allow us to be successful on the playing field?**

* **Are our coaches following the principles and guidelines to become master coaches?**

* **Are our players following the principles and guidelines to become class skillful thinking players?**

* Do we have the style of game to play that will ultimately allow us to be successful on the playing field?

These seven questions will always remain the same, as they are the basis for any organisation, irrespective of their size, who wants to gain winning results on the field.

Who are more important?

*People who can
fix things in a crisis*

or

*People who can
make things run smooth?*

Growing
Flowers

*The true leaders of today
are Building
the base of tomorrow*

Making it to the Top

There are two ways to raise standards to make your way to the top. You can either buy in the best players, coaches and managers or develop the best players, coaches and managers.

Developing your own players, coaches and managers is definitely the cheaper option, though you have to know and understand what you are doing, which is why most people and organisations go towards the buying route to win championships and trophies. By saying the above, **I have set up a conundrum, because if you either do not know how to develop players, coaches and managers or haven't got the cash to buy the talent in how do you expect to get success at the top?**

You can gain short term success buying talent in, though it is the organisations and people who are actively developing their own players, coaches and managers who are the ones that have sustained success at the top.

When getting to the top, sport can be broken into different tiers. You have everybody up to 17th, and then move between 16th to 11th position, then 10th to 7th position, then 5th and 6th position and finally a top 4.

The teams in each tier are battling each other for the top spot in that tier. Occasionally one team in a tier will slip in standards required to stay up.

If their playing standards do drop, and the team does recognize the signs that they are slipping, they do have time to regain their standards before they are past by the next top teams from a lower tier.

As can be seen, if a team does drop the standards required to remain in their tier, then there becomes ample opportunity for a lower tier team to work their way up the playing pyramid.

The teams in the lower tiers have to keep their standards high for when the opportunity arises they have to be prepared to shift up. When the changes do occur, it is not a slow process. The buildup might be a slow process but when the change occurs it can virtually happen in the space of two seasons.

Though I have said there is ample of opportunity to move up, you should also notice that **as you progress up each tier that the going does get harder.** This is because there are less and less spaces to move into the next level. The teams in each level are fighting each other to take out the top spot in each tier.

The above reasons is why it doesn't matter what rules an organisation brings in to regulate a competition to try an even it out, at the end of the day there will always be a top 4 who dominate at anyone time, a top 6 and a top 10, as any competition will naturally revert back to a pyramid structure when sides are reaching for the top.

When you are sitting down to work out how you are going to make it to the top, keep these pointers at the back of your mind as you go through the process of getting better and going higher.

* To break into the top 10 is relatively easy.

* To break into the top 6 requires a different approach.

* To break into the top 4 requires a whole new rethink.

Be aware of the teams that are in the level above you. If they have been there for a while, they'll consider it a right of theirs to be there and if they are allowed to, will play in a way and use tactics to keep the pretenders down and in their place.

If it does happen then you have to be strong and just keep working away at it and when you finally do break through, your standard will be much higher than theirs, and then they'll have to spend their time catching you up.

Building a successful side

In my years of coaching one thing I've discovered is that **if you can get a positive aspect to what you are doing, then players and people who are of a positive disposition will respond accordingly and you can achieve great and unexpected things.** People of a negative disposition will eventually disappear. You may not get the results you want in the short term but in the long run you cannot but succeed.

To build a successful side for the long term, you need a:

* Coach with a positive disposition

* Manager with a positive disposition

* Support staff with a positive disposition

* Players with a positive disposition

* Supporters with a positive disposition

* Positive playing structure (attack and defense)

* Positive training techniques

* Never say die attitude

* Achievements driven

* Everyone involved has or develops the required talents and skills.

You can build a side on negativity and fear but wouldn't it be better to build an environment in which people want to stay or join and be involved in?

I've seen a lot of teams under achieve because their coach is driving them from a negative angle. They berate their players and drive them into the ground. The players only perform because they're too scared of the consequences if they don't.

Thankfully I haven't been involved with too many sides as a player, when the coach has been like that. After having seen negative coach's in action and listening to the players and parents and hearing what they say, I guess its coloured my way of looking at things.

I'm also a believer that if people get on together and actively work on making it happen, then you can achieve wonderful results.

Two of the teams I worked with, that went really well, both were rep sides and ended up in the top two at their particular tournaments. Even though we didn't take the top prize, and weren't really expected to, we surprised a lot of people at what we achieved and created a buzz with the side that spread through the player's, spectators and the tournament administrators.

It's great when everything starts to come together and creates a great feeling that goes with it and still be successful as well. It's a shame that more people don't experience it.

Hardest thing to admit in coaching

One of the hardest things as a coach is to admit to your self that *"I do not know, or I do not understand"*. **One way to keep discovering new things is to keep a child like ability to be able to question so you can increase your understanding.** As people grow older, a majority lose that ability. You need that child like curiosity in you to be maintained and turned towards the adults unknown. **The simplest of questions can lead to the most soul searching of answers.**

With coaching there is one major point you have to accept, that the better you get, the more the opposition will try to prevent you from succeeding until there comes a point where their efforts to stop you is succeeded by your ability to beat them, unless you give up first.

One area we let ourselves down badly as clubs and associations is in our inability to develop our coaches. We get so blinded to the fact it is players who play the game, which is right, that we tend to forget that the people doing the real thinking and planning to put the players out on the park and who has a truer understanding of the game are the coaches.

Coaches have to take some of the blame for this because we tend to start hogging information and don't want to give away secrets to our success but as we all know the game keeps changing so we have to keep up with the play. Finding the information is the easier part, putting it together so that it works for what you are doing, now that's a tough one and that's where the real art in coaching comes into it.

Four points which will enable coaches to keep developing:

* Regardless of numbers, maintain standards

* Look for patterns rather than only events and forces to react to

* Focus on performance rather than results

* Keep workloads to a manageable level

(Principal of the more work you do, the more work there is to do)

To be a successful Coach you need to be:

* Innovative

* Creative

* Flexible

* Adaptable

* Passionate

* Observant

* Analytical

* Able to think outside the square

* Asks questions – who, what, why, where and how?

* Do not take things at face value

* Constantly updating knowledge

* Prepared to take risks

* Not afraid to have the occasional disappointments

* Able to look at other sports and adapt their ideas

* Challenge your own thinking

* Can swap ideas

As you come up with ideas what you need to do is to expand your knowledge to see if you still come to the same conclusions, in other words: **Observe, apply, and learn.**

Types of players

In my years of coaching I have noticed you can group players into three types. All three have a part to play in sport and the more you can develop the third type of player, the more successful you will become. The player types are as follows:

Journey Man

Is a person who can perform the same job for a position on the field over and over again but doesn't have the skill level required to break open a game. They are very good at reading the play and putting them selves in position early. Generally have very good self discipline because they have to apply themselves to succeed at any level.

Skilled Player

Is a person who has the skill level to break open a game, but is unable for the duration of a game to perform the same job over and over again in the position that they are playing. Tend to be lacking in self discipline. Very good hand eye co ordination. Not the kind of person you want in defence unless they can develop their self discipline. They tend to gravitate to the points scoring part of the game.

Class Skillful Thinking Player

This person can perform the same job for a position over and over again, who can perform the basics of the game at a high level and has the skill level to break open a game.

These players put them selves in a position on the field to use their basics most of the time, thus giving the appearance they have time and make things look easy. If they don't use their skills in a game, it doesn't worry them; maybe the game didn't warrant it. Because these players have time, their thinking is a lot clearer on the field.

Because someone is skillful and talented

Doesn't mean the brains and maturity came with them

Releasing potential in players

We've all seen it in sport, players who had the potential to go a long way in whatever they choose, but for some reason, that potential is never realized. They may succeed at a certain level but their potential and sporting talent is never fully realized. In other words, these players are selling themselves short.

Conversely, we have all seen other players go further with less talent and skill. Some how they have tapped into their reserve of potential to make the most of what they have got.

In my many discussions with people, one day I was having a conversation and we were talking about a player in the team, when the person I was talking to asked me, *"How long does it take to develop potential in a player?"*

Without hesitation I answered back, *"2 years."* Then he said, *"Why have we been mucking around with this player for 4 years then."*

This question and the answer I gave got me to thinking, **what is the makeup of potential and how do you develop potential in players?**

When you are saying someone has got potential, you are saying they have got a talent and skill for a sport, but they aren't utilizing it in a way to get the best out of themselves, at the highest level that they could play.

How do you draw out potential?

It revolves around the individual and the reason it can take 2 years to develop potential, is because a player has to cultivate their self discipline and develop a work ethic.

This means you are looking at altering behaviour patterns in people, and essentially they will be learning new skills. This takes time, and as we know, behavioural change doesn't occur over night. It takes both persistence and constant working at.

A person with a talent for a sport, eg: their natural hand eye and muscle co ordination has the ability to release and make the most of their potential sooner, than a person with less talent available to them. **What talent does is it enables you to start at a higher level than a person with less talent and allows you to the higher level quicker, if you put in the work.**

You are also looking at working on the sports basics and key skills, which requires repetition. Unfortunately the less self discipline and work ethic that people have, the less work on the basics/key skills they will actually do. So the chance of developing their potential is reduced.

We've all seen some one who has a great talent, and maybe playing at a high level, but their true and full potential is never realized because they are getting by on their talent alone, whereas some one with less talent, who plays at the same level, but has greater self discipline and an excellent work ethic will be getting the most out of themselves and playing to their truer potential than the first person.

Both players can still get better.

If the above players want to improve and play at a higher level, the first person needs to go away and cultivate their self discipline and work ethic and spend more time on their basics/key skills, as well as working on the rest of their game.

The second person would spend more time on his co ordination and skills to enhance on their excellent self discipline and work ethic, as well as continuing to work on their basics/key skills.

Therefore, for a player to bring out their potential and play to their true level, they have to:

* **Cultivate their self discipline**

* **Develop an excellent work ethic**

* **Work on the basics and key skills of their sport**

And to carry on improving, by continuing to work on and develop the rest of their game.

Develop Class Players

There are three things a player needs to become a class player. They are:

* **Self Discipline**

* **Repetition of the basics and key skills**

* **Expand and improve on their skill base**

The big one of the lot is self discipline, for with out self discipline you'll never develop a class player, because, to become a class player you have to be able to do the three R's, they being:

* **Repetition**

* **Repetition**

* **Repetition**

To be able to do the repetition you have to take pride and satisfaction in doing the simple things well and doing a job well done.

So essentially in what ever you do, you want to:

* **Keep it simple**

And then do:

* **The simple things well over and over again**

By doing the above, you'll be on your way to develop class in players.

What is Self Discipline?

How often have you set some of your players a task, say we are going to be doing it for the next 10 minutes. You leave them to it after they get it going because you need to work with some other players on another task. After 5 minutes you look back at the original group and they are changing the way they do the skills or are doing something else.

All Self Discipline is, is the ability to self motivate your self to complete a task and complete it over and over again without having to be constantly watched or being checked upon periodically to make sure you are doing what is required.

If you are hearing, I'm always being watched, or people are always checking up on me. It's always an indication that self discipline is not high in their priority or it's not as good as it should be. The sooner you cultivate your self discipline; the sooner people will stop watching over you. **If people cotton onto the benefits of self discipline,** then it opens up a whole new world to them and a whole world of opportunities, which you don't get until you cultivate your self discipline.

The other aspect that compliments self discipline is mental maturity.

People who have a high level of mental maturity generally:

* Take responsibility for them selves and their actions

* Apply any wisdom and knowledge learned

* Develop a grounded personality

* Display signs of leadership

This side of a player's preparation is generally overlooked, but it is what sets apart the successful from the talented. I have seen many a talented person not achieve to the level that they should because they are missing the two vital pieces of self discipline and mental maturity out of their make up and do not attempt to work on them.

Player Turnover

We all hear about it, we'd all be so much better off if we didn't keep losing players. Or we're from a small area and we always keep losing players.

In reality, player turnover happens to everybody, everywhere, all the time, regardless of the area or club size.

Here are a few points worth considering. If you can keep these in mind, then you can start planning for the changes which happen each year.

Points to Consider

* A new generation of players will come through approximately every 10 years.

* At some point there is a two to three year cross over period between generations.

* How do you make the crossover continuous between generations (clue: Development Structure)

* Basically you are looking at replacing at least two players every year.

* When a team hits an invincible run without a change in personal, by dominating the opposition and having a run of no losses, it will generally last two years,(especially at international level), before there starts to be the need for a change in personal.

After the two years if there is no change in personal, the longer the delay the longer it will take to attain the same sort of level back up to the top.

I have lived in an area that can go through periods of high turn over with players. The senior team I coached, one time, within the space of 3 years, I only had 3 of the same people left to work with and one of them was me. In that time we still managed to stay at the top of the competition and win trophies.

Also **many years ago I decided I wasn't going to wait for talented players to come along to get success,** so I decided to develop a system that would make the most of what we had and when talented players came along, then that would be a bonus.

Subsequently when you get involved with age group teams, if you stay at a particular age group, you only get to work with the players for a couple of years. So if you want to be good, you have to develop a system to bring players on very quickly but also very safely. You don't want to bring them on to burn them out.

Another way you can get success at age group level is to start with a side at a young age and when they shift into the next age group, move through with them, so you get more time to work with them. That way you do not have to worry too much about player turnover.

Playing Structure

To have an effective playing structure, players have certain roles and jobs they have to perform, and certain areas they have to be on the field in relation to the position they are playing.

As long as the players are fulfilling the basic and minimum requirements of their positions within the structure being played, then they are free to add their own personal touches, attributes and skills to their positions to make it their own, but never at the expense of the basic minimums required for their positions.

A lot of people get hooked up with playing structures and systems and start trumpeting the virtues of the one they use. In reality it comes down to what you want to achieve on the field, how you want to control the opposition, keep their dangerous players quiet and whether you want to be positive or negative on the field.

One area that gets overlooked with a playing structure concerns player positioning away from and not directly involved with the immediate play as they have a big influence on the success or otherwise of the team as they determine how well the defensive structure will operate or as outlets to create an attack.

To have an effective playing structure you will need a system.

What is a system? Broken down, simply it is the way something is done or the process used to achieve an aim. For example, two people may have the same aims, but the way they do things, (or the systems they use) maybe different.

For example in most field sports you want to run a structure which

* Congests the midfield, forcing the opposition wide.

* Cuts out angled and flat cross field passes, thereby literally slowing down and restricting the opposition to one side of the field.

* Flexible enough that when your team has the ball they can change from defense into attack in the shortest period possible.

* Able to switch play and the point of attack with numbers still available in defense and able to cover.

When playing an opposition, **a dangerous team is one which can switch play and their point of attack at any given time**, so you will be looking to run a system or structure to prevent it from happening but also allowing yourself to switch the play and point of attack at any given time.

There are two key areas for having an effective playing structure. They are organization and communication.

Without either, any structure will break down regardless of how good it is.

At the end of the day, what structure and system you use is up to you. Have a look at all the systems and structures that are played for your sport or borrow some from others, and see which works for your situation.

As long as you know how the system you use works and can explain it to your players and they go out onto the field and make it happen, for that is the ultimate test.

Learning verses Practice

There are three parts to getting better at what you do. You have a learning phase, a practice phase and a develop phase.

The starting point is obviously the learning phase. You try the skill to begin with and learn all the different parts and how they fit together. Then you practice what you have learnt. As you practice you get more efficient and better at the skill. At some stage you will learn a new technique or get better information so you develop the skill further; effectively you go back into a learning phase.

After you develop the skill further, you have to go back and practice it to become efficient and better at it. You have to keep practicing the skills to be excellent at them. For example, a concert pianist doesn't stop practicing a piece of music once they know it. They keep practicing the piece of music so they stay excellent at it.

When you are practicing, you are strengthening the neural pathways and developing the muscle memory associated with performing the skills.

The way to develop both is by repetition. Repetition also develops self discipline.

People can go *"practicing is boring"* or more specifically they mean the repetition. If people find the repetition in general boring, it means they are lacking the self discipline to apply themselves to the task at hand. There are ways and means to make repetition interesting. It is up to you as a coach to work that one out and to get the balance between practicing, learning and developing right.

The reason trainings are called practice is because you are practicing the skills required to play the game. You are not learning or developing the skill. You are practicing the skill. What happens is people end up developing all the time and do not actually end up practicing.

If you are constantly learning or developing skills and not practicing them, you will keep improving, but you will not become efficient at executing the skills.

Realistically, if you break it down, we should be saying to our players, at today's training we shall be doing learning of a skill, or at today's training we shall be doing practice of a skill or at today's training we shall be doing development of a skill. At the moment we lump everything under the term practice. This is where the confusion is happening because we are doing the different phases all under the same name.

With sport, the majority of your training time will be taken up with practicing the skills learnt and developed, especially if preparing for tournaments and finals.

When it comes to learning, information is taken in through the conscious mind which enables you to start putting it into and programming the subconscious mind. Programming the subconscious is done differently for each person. Some can pick up a new skill by looking, others by going through the action, others by being talked to about it, others having to ask questions which helps to build pictures in their head about what is to be achieved. The way the person learns, is the way they program the skills or information into their subconscious.

The reason you want a skill in the subconscious is because that is where all the best performances happen from. The reason the best performances occur when working from there is **the subconscious mind doesn't take the time to think, the conscious mind does.** In higher competitions you have less time to think, because events are happening so much quicker.

When it comes to game time, accessing the subconscious is done by setting up a program in the conscious mind which enables access to the subconscious mind, the neural pathways and muscle memory of the skills. **You want to be able to perform the skills by eliminating outside pressure and without the conscious mind disrupting the process for executing the skills.**

This is why you need to practice the skills, so you can strengthen the neural pathways and develop muscle memory, so during a game when executing the required skills, you don't have to stop and think about how to do them.

Expand your skill base, Sharpen your basics

As you move higher through the grades and playing levels, it stands to reason that you have to expand your skill base if you want to compete and ultimately get better.

By developing and expanding your skill base you start giving yourself more time on the playing field. **With more time you can perform the basics of your sport more accurately during a game.** What normally happens as people develop more time on the playing field is they start looking to execute all the difficult skills during a game. This might look spectacular, flamboyant and exciting **but when the pressure goes on; the mistake level goes up and the accuracy drops.**

So you get to practice and people get in and start expanding their skill base and they become so preoccupied with it that they neglect their basics. The reason why you need to keep working on and perfecting the basics, is, as you go higher and higher through each playing level, the need to eliminate technical mistakes and improve your accuracy becomes more important, because, **you have to make less mistakes to win the crucial games**. At the top level, a missed trap, a dropped catch or an inaccurate pass at the wrong time can be the difference between winning and not winning.

Do not get me wrong, there is a time and a place to use the flamboyant skills and players will get ample time to display them in a game.

As you get near the top of any level you need to sharpen your basics because the competition is tighter so you need to make fewer mistakes. Once you get through to the next level, you have to expand on your skill base or improve the ones you've got, and then as you approach near the top of that level you have to sharpen your basics. So the process of improving becomes a constant cycle of expanding and improving your skill base and continually sharpening your basics.

For as you expand and improve your skill base you are always creating room for sharpening your basics.

*The difference between being
positive or negative
is a state of mind*

Part 3

Attain
Your Aims

The
Steps
To Success

Life is only as complicated
As you organize it

This section is for people who want to learn how to develop their own ideas and to learn of the process that goes into the development of concepts and how to be successful.

There are principles to be successful and at the turn of the 19th century, people were writing about them. They include Wallace Wattles, James Allen, Charles F Haanel, William Walker Atkinson, and the most successful and well known of them all, Napoleon Hill.

The principles to succeed they wrote about are as relevant today as they were back then. The writers of today, such as Jack Canfield, Tony Robbins and Bob Proctor are putting these same principles into today's language.

Essentially what they have all written is:

* Have an idea or picture in your head to aim to; the more vivid you make it the better.

* Have a focus and a desire to achieve your aim.

* Allow your sub conscious to work on the picture.

* Capture and make use of the ideas that surface from your sub conscious.

* Take action that will move you towards your aim or picture.

* Keep going until you succeed.

The principles have always been there, they always will be.

They obviously have written much more, but at its essential level, that's it. I would recommend reading their work to learn more. The following few pages is my take on how I have interpreted these principles for my own understanding and applied them to sport.

*The information you require
to succeed is there,*

It is up to you to seek.

The Process

The process you go through if you want to develop something or achieve anything is to begin with an aim.

For example, the teams that I coach, I want them to play the best type of hockey that they can, irrespective of their age. That is my aim. My first task was to begin looking round at the most successful teams and with the benefit of television, got to watch many games from overseas and many different sports and I started studying how they were playing.

What I noticed and by using inductive reasoning, was that **the same type and style of game was being played by those who were successful over a period of time, regardless of the sport played.**

As you will be aware by now, the type of game that came to the fore is a flowing game and the style of game they play is a passing game through the midfield.

Coming to the conclusion that **a passing game and a flowing game is the one to play to be successful over a period of time,** I then began the task of gathering information. So I asked myself and other people some questions, as well as looking at books, magazines and on the internet.

Some of the questions I asked were:

* How do they do it?

* What do they do at training?

* What type of player do they develop?

* What's their thinking process during a game?

* What skills are needed?

* Can everything be replicated and if so can it be taught?

* If it can be taught, how do you teach it?

You just keep asking and asking and asking, and **the better the quality the questions, the better the quality the answers.**

Once you've asked the questions, then you've got to start looking for the answers and begin researching and trialing and making errors.

I've never known anyone to attempt a project and not make a mistake; it's the nature of learning. So you try things, if it works keep it, if it doesn't, get rid of it. So it becomes a process of building on to the things that keep working and taking you towards your aim.

As you are working along, you have to organize your information, and put it in a way that you can replicate it from year to year. It's also advantageous if you write it down, as this helps to clarify your thinking and makes you examine your own theories, concepts and ideas.

If you want to go the next step, which most people don't, you can always present your information in presentations or articles and show them to people to get their feed back. This is another way to test to see if what you are doing is sound and whether you are on the right track or heading off on a tangent.

Put this process together with developing vision and you never know what you might end up creating. I certainly didn't when I began on this journey.

Developing vision

When reading a lot of manuals and books on playing sport, the authors give you all the drills and theories on playing whose ever game they are writing about, without ever saying what they were or are trying to achieve.

As previously mentioned, what you will find behind all the drills and theories most of **the top coaches will have some sort of vision or big picture that they are working to and want to achieve.** This gives direction and will dictate what types of drills are used to achieve.

So what is this vision or big picture, and if it so important, why hasn't it been talked or discussed about much before??

I think vision has been given a mystical type quality, whereas to me **vision is the ability to be able to see (visualize) a realistic picture of what is possible and can be achieved in the future, which is different and above the current reality.** This aim is such a small part of the equation that most people don't see or understand the importance of having one.

A slight warning is needed here, what may be one person's possibility can seem pie in the sky to the majority, so be prepared for derision and put downs if you are going to go on this path.

The trick to achieving your vision is to work out and implement the correct steps to attain it.

You also might have the vision or big picture but you may have to enlist the help of extra people to work out the steps required to get there.

When developing your vision it is figuratively better to be looking from the outside in as this gives a better overall picture.

How do I develop my own vision?

1. Establish what level you are currently working at.

2. Decide what you think you can achieve. (it may have to be adjusted accordingly)

3. Once you have decided what can be achieved decide what type of game or style is required to reach that level. (it may take some research or observation of good teams)

4. Develop a philosophy to link your current reality to your vision.

5. Once you have settled on a philosophy, next decide what steps are required to reach your vision.

6. Develop drills along your philosophy to enable you to reach your required level set out.

7. Evaluate constantly, you may have to adjust your drills, philosophy or steps to reach your initial vision.

8. This whole sequence is a process which may take an extended period of time.

9. Develop a thick skin and open mind, you'll need the thick skin for all the derision and put downs which is sure to come your way. You also need an open mind because; you never know where the next idea to take you forward is going to come from or what that idea may be.

10. Once you have reached or are approaching your initial vision, start planning your next.

11. Have faith and belief in your own convictions.

Practical example of the use of vision to progress

1. Current Level

Team with no understanding of structure, no attacking ability, good defense, limited attack options, constantly being beaten, no playing consistency.

2. What can be achieved?

We are competitive and play against all the teams in the local competition with great attacking skill and defensive structure.

3. Game style

Based on getting the basics right, plenty of short passing, positional game, plenty of supporting the ball carrier, players running into space, create time and space by using skills, deny the opposition time and space by pressuring the ball carrier and his support players.

4. Philosophy to achieve

To build up a players and teams skill base so they have more time, space and confidence to execute the basics with speed and intensity when put under pressure situations.

5. Steps to achieve

Understand how the game works, develop drills required to achieve vision, get off the bottom of the table, start scoring goals, start beating the teams immediately above us then proceed to the teams at the top of the table, make defensive structure better able to support attack, learn the mechanics of and how to score goals.

Another example of the use of vision to progress

1. Current Level

Teams I am taking are achieving and winning trophies at a local regional level.

2. What can be achieved?

My teams are successful and winning at national level and all players have the ability to play for the national side.

3. Game style

The game style is based on a flowing game with accurate passing through the midfield, being executed by class skillful thinking players. My teams will be sound and solid in defence and efficient and effective in goal scoring. My teams and players will display all the other attributes as outlined in my playing picture.

4. Philosophy to achieve

The more I understand and know, the simpler and more effective I can make it, and therefore bring the players to the required standard quicker which will keep the continuity going for the team's continued success.

5. Steps to achieve

Get the players to want to improve. Get the players to raise their standards and have them strive to reach higher. I will implement the training structures and systems to achieve success.

Let your mind do the thinking

If you want to succeed, all the intricate information required for breakthroughs that you need to know or use is out there. It is up to the individuals involved in their particular field to be able to tune into or notice these intricacies but is generally out of the range of most people's radars.

The way people notice these intricacies is by focusing on and having a desire for what they want to achieve. If they do, then people start to pick upon the odd or fluctuating information in their peripheral thinking. This significant information in their peripheral is missed by most people as their signal is so weak, that without any focus, we don't register them.

For those who are able to tune into these signals and are inquisitive by nature, find this information in the corner of their thoughts fascinating so they start to look more closely at them. Be aware, **the information doesn't come to you; you have to go to it.** If you lose the focus and desire, the information drifts away and goes back to be hidden in the general clutter.

People who have the ability to focus and tune into these signals can see the significance of this information, because **when you focus your attention, the strength of the signals is the most brightest and loudest amongst the dullness of the general clutter.** To also make sense of this information, people who tune into it need to be able to decode what they receive, for it can come out randomly and in parts, and then be able to interpret it for the mainstream until they are able to understand it as well. By the time the mainstream have come up to this point, the people who have originally spotted this information have long gone and are working on other intricacies they have tuned into.

When you focus and tune in to this information, your subconscious is paying attention via your eyes and ears all the time and then it is up to you to use your conscious mind to ask the right questions. Your subconscious mind will act on these questions and then goes through and sorts out and throws any thoughts to your conscious mind, at any time.

It is important to write these thoughts down, play with and add to them, so they can be added back to the subconscious and worked and expanded upon to come up with a better result. The following are some general guidelines and attributes for the type of person who has the ability to tune into these signals of information.

* Working to an aim or plan

* Asks themselves and others lots of questions

* Have a particular focus and passion in their field of expertise

* Broad range of interest

* Inquisitive

* Observant

* Analytical

* Initially not the top achievers

* Have an open mind

* Have philosophies and guidelines

* Generally flies under the radar until results start to be achieved

* Able to spot the odd or unusual which would normally be missed

* Asks after and looks for information not already knowingly recorded or documented

* Ability to see underlying patterns and reoccurrences of events

* Have perception

*Able to simplify the complicated

* Does not accept that the current way is the best way

Change

Have you ever sat down and wondered about change and why we don't stay still or in the same place for long?

The following explanation may help you to understand why at some stage we must take the decision and figuratively set sail for a new destination so we don't become overtaken if we are in business or sport and would like to remain at or near the top and why what worked for us yesterday may not sustain us today. To explain the following I'll use sport as an example, but this could easily be applied to anything you want.

If you imagine all the information that we have access to as being a sea and all of the teams that are at or near the top being on an island to put them above the sea level and above the competition, thus giving them an advantage. The rest of the teams that make up the numbers are on boats floating around this sea, thus they haven't got the advantage of being above sea level. **The reason why we get change** is that any new information eventually gets added to this sea of information, so in effect what happens is the sea level is constantly rising, sometimes subtlety, sometimes in a rush.

What can happen is that **the top teams can gain a false sense of security by being on these islands,** so what sometimes happens is they build walls around themselves for added security to remain on top. This is setting them up for failure in the future for when the sea rises they don't see the changes happening. What the problem becomes is that if they need to re launch to find another advantage island and because some people may not know any other way of working they face the difficult decision of change. Some teams or organisations may have been on one of these islands for a number of years.

If you are one of these teams which are merely floating around the sea, you maybe asking, **how can we get to one of these islands?** This is where some of the previous pages come into play; **it comes down to developing vision and let your mind do the thinking.** Not many people can see these islands and that is why some get called crackpots, eccentrics, nutters or they just not living on this planet.

Also not all islands are the same, some maybe only small which gain you an advantage for a short time and some maybe so large that by the time you have to change, that the person or people who got you there are no longer around and you're left wondering what to do.

If you do make it to one of these islands the next step is to enjoy the initial success while you are there, but what must be done next is to start preparing for the next bout of change. As we have seen it will come and then actually make the decision at some stage to re launch and be brave enough to chart a course to the next advantage island.

To re launch is much easier than it sounds for if the pickings are still easy on the island you are on then there will be a major reluctance by the majority to re launch.

Preparation is the best key because at some stage you will have to go. What is ironical is that the larger islands that people crave are the harder ones to see as they are further away and it is why you need people of vision to help you get there, but the irony of this is unless recognized, these are the people who are the first to get ridiculed or persecuted for their ideas.

In general there are different types of information seas. You've got your sciences, business, sport, communities, and arts. The list is endless. These lists can be broken down further to their specific fields of expertise, for example, sport can be broken down to rugby, soccer, hockey, netball, and boxing, the list goes on. I hope what I have written does help; it may even be a bit out there for some, but if it has helped you'll start looking at things from a different angle and gain an appreciation on why things will constantly change.

At the end of the day you have got two choices. You can either drift and let the currents take you and end up where you may and be happy with limited results, or you can set a course and focus on your destination and target and work your way there.

To achieve your destination, you may have to go against a head wind, by which I mean the current held belief, and if you have faith in what you are doing and keep tacking and heading to where you are going, you'll eventually get there.

The
Final Whistle

*Those that learn the least
are the ones that need
to learn the most*

Thank you

I am grateful to have had this opportunity to pass this information on and I would like to thank every one who has taken the time to read this book.

I would also like to thank everybody who has helped me over the years and I am forever grateful to your contribution. There are too many people to individually thank and I know in your own heart, you know who you are.

I'm sure I must have annoyed a few of them over the years as I tried to work on issues that had me perplexed and I kept visiting them until I had worked out and tested each part.

The only thing I have done is to set out the principles and guidelines that people need to follow if they want to be a winning coach and prepare a side or individual to success.

If you look at it, the principles for building a Rolls Royce are the same ones for building a mini.

It's the same for sport; the principles for succeeding at a high level are the same ones you need to follow to succeed at a low level. The execution is the only difference.

To all who follow this sporting philosophy, I will toast your success.

If sport is your passion, let this book be your guide.

The people who go on to become winning coaches and prepare winning teams have:

* A playing aim and an ideal picture of the way their sport is to be played

* A list of key skills and their techniques and practice them

* Get the best out of their players

* Develop a brain for their sport

* Have a recipe or method for putting it all together

And aim towards the following three things:

Type of game to play:

A Positive Flowing game.

The style of game they play through the midfield:

A Controlled Short Passing game.

The types of player they develop are:

Class Skillful Thinking Players.

And have an accurate description for the way they want their team to play on the field.